Theodore Andrea Cook

Old Touraine

The Life and History of the Famous Chateaux of France: Vol. II

Theodore Andrea Cook

Old Touraine
The Life and History of the Famous Chateaux of France: Vol. II

ISBN/EAN: 9783337191382

Printed in Europe, USA, Canada, Australia, Japan

Cover: Foto ©ninafisch / pixelio.de

More available books at **www.hansebooks.com**

OLD TOURAINE

THE LIFE AND HISTORY OF
THE FAMOUS CHATEAUX OF FRANCE

BY

THEODORE ANDREA COOK, B.A.

SOMETIME SCHOLAR OF WADHAM COLLEGE, OXFORD

IN TWO VOLUMES

VOL. II

Second Edition, Revised

CHARLES SCRIBNER'S SONS

743 and 745 BROADWAY

New York

1893

CONTENTS

CHAPTER XIII

CHAPTER XIV

CHAPTER XV

CHAPTER XVI

CHAPTER XXIII

LIST OF ILLUSTRATIONS

CHENONCEAUX (*Continued*)

IN the gossip with which the pages of Brantôme are filled, the Court of Henry II. lives for us in all its details. We can see the King showing his stables to the Emperor's ambassador, and parading the young nobles of his suite, " mon autre haras de ces pages que j'estime autant que les autres," or taking him to see the famous greyhounds whose ancestors were brought to Saint Louis from Tartary, and those noble white deerhounds which Charles IX. would recommend as the only breed for a King to take out hunting : we can imagine the day at Court which the observant Venetian ambassador describes, such as it might often have been at Chenonceaux. It is early in the day, but the King, who rose with the sun, has been for some time closeted with De Guise, Vendôme, and the Constable.

MONOGRAM OF HENRY II., in which his name is joined either to that of Catherine de Medicis, or of Diane de Poitiers (taken from the harness of his horse, and the walls of Chenonceaux).

talking over affairs of State in his new-fashioned
" narrow council." After business come devotions,
for the King attends regularly at mass, and after
devotions, dinner ; and now Henry has done with
seriousness for the day—though counsellors and
secretaries are still at work in the great hall of the
castle—and with Saint André by his side he rides
forth a-hunting in the forest of Amboise. Vieilleville
is with them too, talking of affairs at Metz,[1] or
asking for the latest fashions in furniture or food
at his friend's luxurious establishment at Saint
Valéry ; and as the sound of the hunters' horns
grows fainter in the distance, and the western sun
glows on the terraced garden, the walks begin to fill
with the ladies of the Court, in the costumes Cesare
Vecellio has made familiar—small velvet caps with
strings of pearls and feathers, wide slashed sleeves
and flowing robes with a long girdle drooping from
the waist.

M. Ramus may perhaps be there, disputing with
the King's doctor, Fernel, on a knotty point in mathe-
matics, and little thinking that his cruel end shall
come in the massacre of St. Bartholomew, and his
mangled corpse be dragged about the streets of Paris
by bloodthirsty Aristotelians : Jean Daurat helps the
argument with a Greek quotation, and speaks of the

---

[1] See Bertrand de Salignac for the account of the operations of
Claude de Lorraine, Duc de Guise, at Metz, and for much further information see Vieilleville's own *Mémoires*.

promise of his pupil Ronsard with his fellow-country-man Muret, who shall put much sound learning into Montaigne's head. Amyot, too, has left the Dauphin at his studies to have a word with Estienne about some new edition of the classics, or to tell the others to prepare their pretty speeches for Diana, who is just strolling across the drawbridge. This is her first appearance in public, but she has been up long before the rest and ridden early through the dewy fields in the cold morning air, then gone to bed again,[1] and in a graceful deshabille transacted what might come of business, or listened to the latest sonnet from the poets of the Court ; and now she appears at last, fresh and provokingly attractive, ready to stand comparison with the fairest ladies about her, and to throw more energy and life than all the rest into her quiet greeting of the King as he comes back from hunting.

It is the Queen's turn now. She has felt somewhat neglected between the invincible Diana and this new prodigy from Scotland, who has turned the heads of all the courtiers in France ; but the King and all his gentlemen move gaily towards the rooms of Catherine de Medicis, where, among the fascinating smiles and dances of the famous "escadron volant," the day is finished unconcernedly, and the long halberds of the

---

[1] She allowed herself the luxury of a warming-pan, for which we have the authority of M. Nestor Roqueplan, in whose collection that privileged instrument reposes in good company, side by side with the warming-pans of Marie Stuart and Catherine de Medicis.

archers of the guard begin to glisten in the moonlight as they go their rounds, clad in trunk hose
and striped tunics broidered with the royal cipher.
And so Chenonceaux falls into a graceful slumber.
Let Diana sleep sound while she can, for the awaken-
ing is to be rude enough : the first shock came very
unexpectedly.

In 1559, at the fêtes in celebration of the
marriage of Alva and the Princess Elizabeth, the
King had organised a tournament with great magnificence, forgetful of the evil omen with which his
reign began, amid similar scenes of ill-considered
splendour.   Always a good horseman, Henry insisted
on a bout with the young Comte de Lorges, son of
Montgomery of the Scottish Guard.   The trumpets
ceased as they started, Vieilleville tells us, "which
gave us the first trembling presage of the ill that was
to happen ; " they met and broke their lances, when,
as they parted, the King was seen to sway forward
in his saddle—the splinters of De Lorges' lance had
entered his eye beneath the visor of his helmet.   He
was carried out fainting, lingered unconscious for
four days, and only recovered to hand over the
government formally to Catherine de Medicis, and
then die.[1]

With the King's death came the favourite's

---

[1] See the details in Vieilleville of the experiments made (upon the
heads of criminals) by the doctors to try and discover the injury to the
King's eye. Dumas describes the accident in *Les Deux Dianes.*

disgrace. Diana was turned out of Chenonceaux by the Regent Catherine, and given Chaumont in exchange; but it never consoled her for her double grief, and she went to Anet for the rest of her life, where Goujon's statue might remind her of the royal love that she had lost.

The distinguishing marks of Catherine's strange character soon became apparent in her life at Chenonceaux. She had a mania for building, and to her is due the long gallery, raised upon the arches of De l'Orme, which is perhaps the least happy of the additions to the original château; she had, too, with all the bloodthirsty temperament of her race and her antecedents, the true Medici love for fêtes and extravagant revels in this western home, that might have recalled to her the festivals of her childhood on the Arno.[1]

It was not long before one of these great fêtes began. The Court at Amboise had requested a change of atmosphere, for the consequences of a long and persistent massacre of heretics are less pleasant to the well-conducted mind than the encouraging spectacle of executions still in progress, so Catherine took advantage of her opportunity and prepared a magnificent reception for the young King and Queen in her new home.

---

[1] Touraine is a country of strange and varied habitations; if the holes and caverns at Rochecorbon and Saumur suggested Troglodytes, there is in Chenonceaux an equal resemblance to the lake-dwellings of an earlier age.

The Court, we may suppose, had ridden straight southwards from St. Denis hors, and into the main road by the river at La Croix : a little farther on and they were at the turning to their right, which is the beginning of the main drive of the castle.

At the foot of every tree stood knots of women in their holiday attire, wearing great broad-brimmed rustic hats and waving many-coloured ribands, while their husbands and brothers with flags flying and drums beating made a brave show upon the little hill at the entrance to the park :[1] at the end of the long drive before the great court, the royal pair passed beneath a tall triumphal arch reared on four pillars wreathed with ivy, and inscribed "to the Divine Francis," with graceful reference to the seditions lately crushed. Farther on, past a great double fountain, stood two pyramids with Greek inscriptions, the one referring in a brazen way to the utility of a good conscience, the other praising the wakeful habits of Homeric counsellors.[2]

---

[1] See a very rare little book, *Les Triomphes faictz à l'entrée de Françoys II. et de Marye Stuart au chasteau de Chenonceaux le Dymanche, Dernier Jour de Mars* (o.s.), which was published at Tours in small 4to, reprinted by Techener in 1857), probably written by one Antoine le Plessis-Richelieu, Captain of the King's Guards at Amboise. Mézeray describing the conspiracy of Amboise says : "On donna le commandement des Mousquetaires à Cheval à Antoine du Plessis Richelieu, Gentilhomme Poitevin, tout avoué à la maison de Guise." He was called "le Moine" because he had given up Holy Orders for the military profession. His eldest brother, Louis, was ancestor of the famous Cardinal.

[2] "Nous avons été contrains," says Guillaume Bourgeat, the printer

EAST FRONT OF THE CHÂTEAU OF CHENONCEAUX,

showing the wing built across the Cher by Catherine de Medicis; to the right, the château of Catherine Briçonnet.

By now the King was crossing to the higher terrace by a bridge, beneath which countless fish were playing, much to the amusement of the suite, and on the terrace was a great tower, built with many holes, with a bright light within that shone through many-coloured glasses. As he entered the castle an infinity of " fuzées, grenades, et petardes " went off in streams of fire, and " the delighted company heard at the same time the roar of thirty cannons ranged upon the quay, which filled the air with echoes for a long time." The evening was too young yet for all the company to go indoors, and they strolled through the gardens to see the column raised by Primaticcio,[1] " on which was placed a great golden head of Medusa, with parted lips and hair enlaced with snakes," by which was apparently conveyed that " the prudence and wisdom of *Minerva* accompanied the Queen that day." More columns rose in every corner, crowned with morions and arms, and bearing graceful references in weak distichs to the grief of the Queen-mother ; and all the while more and more fireworks went up and fell hissing into the Cher, " so that the very water seemed to burn." Amid the echoes of the last triumphant burst of welcome on the terrace the

of this account at Tours, "d'imprimer les vers grecques en caractères latins, d'autant que n'avions nuls caractères grecs, ce que nous aurons de brief, Dieu aidant."

[1] We can imagine Primaticcio's pleasure at being given the preference over Philibert de l'Orme, his rival, after some years of disfavour.

company moved back past more triumphal arches, and naiads pouring "vin clairet" from their hospitable urns, to the entrance gate, where a Pallas, advancing from the balcony above, rained down a shower of flowers and leaves, inscribed with sonnets to the King and Queen. The very trees for many mornings after, were vocal with rhyming tablets of more or less ill-written greeting.

It is pleasant to think that Marie Stuart must have spent some of the happiest months of her troubled life at Chenonceaux, with the young King, about this time. All Catherine's fêtes had not so fair an excuse. After a reception given to her son the King, Charles IX., in 1565, in the same grounds, she came here again to meet her favourite son, the Duc d'Anjou, who had gone to Chinon after the marriage of Henry of Navarre and Marguerite, and here she heard of Henry's victory of Montcontour, and wished to change the castle's name to " Bonne Nouvelle," without success. In 1577 there was fresh triumph at the Huguenot defeat at Charité-sur-Loire, which had already been celebrated by extravagant orgies at Plessis - lez - Tours ; but Catherine determined to outshine them all, and the pleasant fields of Chenonceaux lent themselves more readily to festivals than the somewhat sombre castle of Louis XI. with all its grim associations.

The King appeared dressed as a woman,[1] with "Master Love" under his arm, no doubt barking at Chicot, and with his "mignons" round him in such enormous ruffs, that "their heads," says the chronicler, "looked like the head of John the Baptist on a charger."

The Queen was there with her daughter Marguerite, and the gentle Louise de Lorraine, and all the flying squadron of her maids of honour, with what little dress they had in flattering imitation of the costume which their masculine admirers had similarly exchanged for petticoats. Brantôme gives the list of all these lively ladies : Mesdemoiselles de Rohan, de Saint André, Davila with stories of the siege of Cyprus, two sisters Gabrielle and Diane d'Estrées, Madame de Sauve, of whom we shall hear more at Blois, and many others. " Tout y estoit en bel ordre," says l'Estoile, so we leave them, with as little scandal as we may, to have their revel out.

Some ten years afterwards the central figure of the fête was dead. Catherine had passed away at Blois, and Henry had been murdered. One of the most unnoticed of the whole throng at the festivals of Catherine came back to Chenonceaux and brought

[1] " Si qu'au premier abord chacun estoit en peine
S'il voyoit un roy-femme, ou bien un homme-reyne."
See Pierre de l'Estoile, *Journal de Henri III.*

Anthropologists may have noticed a "survival" of these extraordinary freaks of costume in the peculiar fondness of the Bank Holiday revellers of to-day for an interchange of their masculine headgear with the more alluring ornaments of their female friends.

a great change with her.   Louise de Lorraine, of the
great house of the Guises, was of very different
mould from the wicked little Duchesse de Montpensier,
or any of her proud relations—a weak, pure soul, who
spent her life in prayer for her worthless husband,
and "stayed where she was," alone with her grief
and without the comfort of children to help her
bear its burden.   The creditors of Catherine de
Medicis had carried off all that was portable of the
work of Bernard Palissy or the sculptures of the
Italians,[1] and the first days of Louise were busied in
arranging her own "meubles bijoux et livres," of
which the catalogue has been preserved by Prince
Galitzin.   Among the books was a description by
M. Balthasar de Beaujoyeulx (printed in 1582) of
the appearance of Louise at the marriage fêtes of
the Duc de Joyeuse.   This quiet, pure woman, in the
midst of a licentious Court, had a beauty of her own
that shrank from the light of criticism in an outspoken time, and passed easily unnoticed among the
rest.   It is to the Venetian ambassador, as usual,
that we must look for a delicate appreciation of her
character and worth.   "She is full of a sweet simplicity," says Girolamo Lippomano, "which nothing
disturbs save the presence of her lord the King, upon
whom her eyes are always fixed. Her face is
pale and somewhat thin, but she has brilliant

---

[1] See *Les Archives de Chenonceaux*, published by M. l'Abbé
Chevalier, from the original MSS.

eyes and light hair over a pure brow and slight features."

At Chenonceaux she stayed for eleven years, vainly demanding justice from Henry IV.; but the King could not do much; he had but little income either, to bestow on her; but it was not much she spent upon herself. One day when she was Queen, she had only a hundred crowns in the world, and gave them all to a messenger who brought good tidings; and now her small income served her to continue her charity to the families of the poor on the estate. A monument of her care for poor prisoners still survives in her benefactions to several Paris prisons.

During the war she writes to the King, who sometimes came to visit her himself, that the Sieur de Rosny was trampling over all her ground with his horses, to the great detriment of the good people of the country, "que je vous prie vous souvenir, Monsieur, qu'ils me sont vassaulz et tenus pour moi comme enfants très affectionez."

So, between weeping and caring for her tenants, her sad life wears to its end. Visitors come to her occasionally—Marguerite de Valois, or the King with Gabrielle d'Estrées, but none of them satisfies her sense of injustice and her bitter grief. In 1601 she died in the Château de Moulins.

Chenonceaux now passed into the hands of the Duchesse de Mercœur and the Vendôme family, and here, while Richelieu was controlling the destinies of France, and the Three Musketeers were quarrelling with his Eminence's guards, Gaston d'Orléans was entertained at supper while the gay Duc de Beaufort,[1] in despair at all attempts to make her father see a joke, turned to try conversation with his daughter, "la grande Mademoiselle"; here, in 1650, came Mazarin to be reconciled with the Duc de Vendôme; and shortly after, the footsteps of Anne of Austria with her son, Louis XIV., were heard in the gallery which had seen so many beauties, but few so royal and so fair. A trace of this visit was left at Versailles, where some statues taken from Chenonceaux were sent to grace the royal gardens.

The last Duc de Vendôme connected with the château was famous for his ugliness, and when very old, and still uglier if possible than before, he married an extremely plain grand-daughter of the great Condé. Mademoiselle d'Enghien, being unable even in the country to get rid of some of her old habits, was so unfortunate as to drink herself to death.

The romance of Chenonceaux seemed in danger of being utterly crushed, when a fresh reign began with the new attractions of the literary Madame Dupin, to whom the place was sold in 1733 by the Duc de Bourbon, not without great legal disputes, in which the whole process of Diane de Poitiers' elaborate arrangements for possession was brought

---

[1] Known in Paris at the time as the "Roi des Halles."

to light again with a new meaning. One La Ferme had been appointed in the name of the nation as proprietor of Chenonceaux, which was thus considered to be a Crown domain, and there is no little irony in the fact of all Diana's schemes, which profited herself so little, having been the main instrument in proving the inalienable rights of this later owner.

Even the debts of Catherine de Medicis came up for discussion, and it was only when the last of the descendants of her host of creditors had been proved satisfied that M. Claude Dupin, the Fermier-Général, a second Bohier in fact, came to Chenonceaux.

This new proprietor was a friend of Montesquieu, and gathered in his wife's salons the most famous literary celebrities of the day. It was a different kind of life from any that had yet been seen in Chenonceaux. Madame Dupin had a certain intelligent little secretary, who actually had the temerity to fall in love with her, and be gently enough reproved ; it is Jean Jacques Rousseau, who shall become the great man of the company later on. Bernis is there, and Buffon, and Voltaire, and unhappy-looking Diderot, with all the Encyclopædists in his train, exhorting poor Jean Jacques to " continue virtuous, for the state of those who have ceased to be so makes me shudder."

The great Revolution, which owed no little to these last visitors to the château, spared its beauty from the ruin with which it visited so many more illustrious and more noted noble houses. The grand-nephew of Madame Dupin, René, Comte de Villeneuve, died here in 1863, after the castle had had yet another literary visit, from George Sand ; and the last memories of Chenonceaux hark back again to Scotland with its latest owners, M. Pelouze and his wife Madame Wilson, a relative of that Daniel Wilson from Glasgow who in 1789 was Under-Secretary of State to the Minister of Finance in France, and whose descendant has but lately gained a somewhat unenviable notoriety in French politics. The wire of his telephone to Paris still hangs in the gallery of the château.

By Madame Pelouze much was done to restore the ancient glories of Chenonceaux, which had been somewhat dimmed by the neglect of the Vendômes, but the traditional financial embarrassments which seem to have hung about the place ever since the bankruptcy of the Marques, its first owners, have unfortunately reappeared ; the enormous sums spent in decoration, and the splendid fêtes that recalled the galas of the sixteenth century, resulted in the arrival of the creditors again, though for less sums than in the days of Catherine de Medicis.

The château is now in the hands of the Crédit Foncier, who charge their visitors a franc a head—"sic transit gloria "—but much of the beauty and all the interest of Chenonceaux still remain. As we left it we saw a solitary swan that floated in the moat; her white breast cut the mirrored image of the walls, and reminded us strangely of the old times that had passed from them. And indeed the traveller will find much that is worthy of a longer visit here than his guide will probably allow him in this home of beautiful women and gigantic debts. He will not be impressed as by the solid masonry and bulk of Chambord or Langeais, but neither will he be left with the sense of a somewhat too respectable and comfortless blank of tradition and association ; he may not find here all the history that seems incrusted on the very stones of Blois, but he will not see the blood of Guises on the floors: the charm of the place is a more domestic one ; the very attempts at fortification only add to its picturesqueness, and are obviously only meant to do so. It seems built especially for the enjoyment of the brilliant Court favourites who so often were its inmates, and to reflect, in the exuberant fancy and brightness of its architecture, the gaieties which were meant to be habitual within its walls.

The rich decorations of the rooms of Francis I., the windows of the boudoir from which Diane de Poitiers watched for the coming of her royal lover, the pictured faces all along the great gallery upon whose ceiling the light from the waves of the Cher dances in strange flickering fragments, all will impress him with a sense of beauty, and will leave him with a pleasant memory. At Amboise he will see the dark side of the picture, and watch the next act of the drama at the Court of Francis II. and Marie Stuart.

IRONWORK LOCK, showing the initials of Henry III. and his wife, Louise de Lorraine. *From the Collection of M. Lacoste, Rue des Saints Pères, Paris.*

CHAPTER XIV

TWO QUEENS OF FRANCE

" La nef qui disjoint nos amours
N'a eu de moi que la moitié,
    Une part te reste, elle est la tienne,
Je la fie à ton amitié,
    Pour que de l'autre il te souvienne."

THE scene in French history in which the children
of Catherine de Medicis played the leading parts,
and which ended in the capitulation of Paris to
Henry IV., begins with the reign of Francis II.
All the principal characters of the drama either
appear, or are in the near distance. Catherine de
Medicis, the Queen-mother, and the young Queen,
Marie Stuart, will be seen first and most clearly; of
Marguerite de Valois we shall hear more later on,
as of Jeanne d'Albret, Madame de Montpensier, and
the lovely Madame de Sauve, Marquise de Noirmoutier.

The reign of Diane de Poitiers was the beginning
of an influence upon the highest issues of French
politics, of women with far less self-control, with
even less scrupulousness, than Henry's favourite—an

influence mainly Italian in its origin, as has been noticed, and to which was due all the misery and bloodshed which the unbridled passions of such women could not but cause.

Of the men, there appear at this time the first generation of the Guises, the Duke François and the Cardinal de Lorraine, powerful with their niece upon the throne of France, the forerunners of the famous Henri de Guise and the second Cardinal ; Anne de Montmorency, the Constable, is here too, with his nephews the Châtillons ; Antoine of Navarre, father of " le bon Béarnais " ; the first Prince of Condé ; De l'Hôpital, Harlay, and De Thou ;—these make up the more important actors in the drama that is to follow. And upon the scenes, or waiting for their turn, are the maids of honour of Catherine de Medicis, the " mignons " of the future Henry III. ; Besme and Coconnas, the murderers of St. Bartholomew ; the grim perfumer of the Queen-mother, Poltrot, Jacques Clement, and Ravaillac. The literary men stand off from such forbidding company : Ronsard, Montaigne, and Estienne Jodelle, with Beauvais, tutor to the young Prince of Navarre, and many more, are hovering about the Court.

Let us look closer at some of these as they throng to the Louvre, where Catherine and the Guises are staying up the young King for his first attempt at royalty. With the Constable, who is talking to Condé and the King of Navarre, are his nephews, Admiral Coligny and the Colonel d'Andelot, watching the clear, keen face of the Cardinal de Guise, with its quick, cat-like eye and the strange hard turn at the corners of his lip, half hidden in the fair hair of the beard ; beside him is his brother, the brave Captain François, gray of tint and thin in face and body, with light grayish hair, " figure d'aventurier, de parvenu qui voudra parvenir toujours " ; in the midst is the little King with his pale puffed face and flat nose,[1] between the Scotch- woman and the Florentine, whose strong, intelligent head, the true muzzle of the Medicis, becomes all but bestial in the prominent mouth and underhang- ing jowl of later life ; but on the other side, in contrast to the pale Italian, is the lovely Marie, for whose love this half-grown King, distracted at the gift of so much beauty, was to exhaust his feeble strength and die ; for never was there charmer of more power than Marie Stuart. Fortunately we are only concerned with her life in France, and with the later years so fruitful in controversy of her chequered career in Scotland, we have nothing to do.

King James of Scotland had married the daughter of Claude de Lorraine, Duc de Guise, and from the troubles of a country constantly at variance with England, their daughter Marie escaped when quite

---

[1] " Il avait le nez fort camus," says Louis Regnier de la Planche in a passage in which the various weaknesses of the sickly Francis are detailed. Anne the Constable was known as "le camus de Mont- morency," from his flat nose.

young to the shelter of the French Court. There we
hear of her first in 1554, at a fête in the gardens of
St. Germain, where she appeared by the side of the
pretty Miss Fleming. Authentic portraits of her a
few years later show her with the auburn-tinted hair
and the fine transparent skin of the painting at Azay-
le-Rideau, the complexion she shared with her uncle
the Cardinal, and a quick, light eye of brownish
tinge that could be hard and fixed at will ; but
her youthful beauty, which was undeniable at this
time at any rate, was the least among her charms.
" Showing an astonishing acquaintance," says Michelet,
" with books, affairs, and men, well versed in politics
at ten, and mistress of the French Court at fifteen,
she ruled everything by her word, by the charm of
her presence, which troubled every heart. In this
wonder, whom the Guises brought to France, every
human gift was united save self-control and tact ;
fantastic and visionary, for all her keenness in
intrigue, for all her seeming cunning and finesse, she
ended by falling into every snare her enemies spread
for her." [1]

[1] It is interesting to note French opinion on her character from
another point of view.

"L'ennemie la plus intime," says Balzac, "et la plus habile de
Catherine de Médicis était sa belle-fille la reine Marie, petite blonde,
malicieuse comme une soubrette, fière comme une Stuart qui portait
trois couronnes, instruite comme un vieux savant, espiègle comme une
pensionnaire de convent, amoureuse de son mari comme une courtisane
l'est de son amant, dévouée à ses oncles qu'elle admirait, et heureuse
de voir le roi François partager, elle y aidant, la bonne opinion qu'elle
avait d'eux."—*Études Philosophiques sur Catherine de Médicis*, p. 90.

MARIE STUART, from the miniature painted by Jackson in 1815, in the possession of A. Stowe, Esquire, Wadham College, Oxford, a copy of the original once in the Bodleian Gallery (see Appendix).

Yet during the few months of her power in France, a power that has been too little recognised, no one could escape her influence, the Queen-mother no more than the rest. A little court of poets gathered round her, Du Bellay and De Maison Fleur [1] among them, whose verses were answered with her own, and gave yet another charm to such memories as those of Chenonceaux. She left France with the sorrow for her young dead husband in her heart, and the sweet verses of her favourite Ronsard in her memory, verses in which for once the poet forgot to be classical and gave utterance to a natural beauty of pathos and expression, but too rare in his writings.

" Adieu," she cries, upon the deck of the ship that bore her from Calais. " Adieu donc, ma chère France, je ne vous verrai jamais plus." The words of Béranger are too true—

> " Adieu, charmant pays de France,
> Que je dois tant cherir ;
> Berceau de mon heureuse enfance,
> Adieu, te quitter c'est mourir."

She left a country where she was always regretted, and which kept a romantic memory of her beauty, a tender pity for her sorrows. The Guises could make no motion at her death, for they were paralysed by

---

[1] Not so well known as his companions ; he was a Huguenot writer of some celebrity in his time, author of *Les Divins Cantiques*, Anvers, 1580.

the murder of Le Balafré, but the French Court had done its utmost to save the victim of its plots with Scotland, and the whole country felt the compassion for her misfortunes, which makes Brantôme's account rise above the ordinary level of a gossiping Court chronicle.

" This Queen," says Giovanni Correro eight years afterwards, " while she kept the love of her honour and the fear of God before her eyes, reigned in a most admirable manner, so that all the world wondered to see a young girl, so delicately nurtured and so little used to government, able to resist the influences against her. The Pope especially favoured her, sending her encouragement with words and money. But her joy was short-lived ; at one blow she lost her husband, her freedom, and her crown."

" Tout ce qui est de beau ne se garde longtemps,"

sings Ronsard,

" Les roses et les lis ne règnent qu'un printemps,
Ainsi vostre beauté, seulement apparue
Quinze ou seize ans en France est soudain disparue."[1]

She left France and the intrigues of the decaying dynasty of the Valois for a rude atmosphere where stronger wills than hers were paramount, and

[1] Malherbe's improvement on these lines ran as follows :—

" Elle était de ce monde où les plus belles choses
Ont le pire destin ;
Et, rose, elle a vécu ce que vivent les roses
L'espace d'un matin."

where she had no longer strength to fight against necessity.[1]

Of very different mould is the woman standing near her by the King's chair. It becomes necessary to have a clear idea of the character which dominates the next thirty years of French history, and who, in 1533, left the intrigues of Italy, to contaminate the French Court.

About Catherine de Medicis at least, there can be no doubt as to the verdict, and even the brilliant attempt of Balzac cannot change the judgment of posterity on one of the most infamous women who ever held the royal power.

The present school of historical criticism, if it delights in destroying old ideals, has shown itself no less skilful at whitewashing characters hitherto condemned without appeal ; and in many cases a fairer estimate of results has been arrived at ; but difficult as it is to accept even a modified picture of the villainies of a Louis XI., it becomes impossible to acquiesce in the strained attempt after originality and paradox, which becomes obvious in any apology for Catherine ; nor will the well-worn argument of the dangers of her situation or the habits of her time suffice to clear her character. Such arguments might have been used in her favour, were her acts, her

---

[1] " L'Angleterre impie," cries Dumas, " ce bourreau fatal de tout ce que la France eut de divin, tua avec elle la grâce, comme elle avait déjà tué l'inspiration en Jeanne d'Arc, comme elle devait tuer en Napoléon le génie."

policy, and her influence other than they are—in the face of results they become absolutely untenable. Nor is it merely a wholesale feeling of disgust at the tendencies and methods of the age, that leads us unequivocally to condemn one of its chief personages. Of the three Queens of that time it was given to but one to succeed, and in her success to build up the greatness of the English nation. The unhappy fate of Marie Stuart has procured a pardon for her faults, the death of Catherine de Medicis was welcomed as a release from an ever-present evil, as the beginning of an attempt to better things. The lives of Coligny, of Jeanne d'Albret, of Henry of Navarre, of Michel de l'Hôpital, show that even in the sixteenth century it was possible to fulfil many duties, many obligations, without the stain of lying or of murder.[1]

[1] Of contemporary authorities perhaps the most severe criticism is the *Discours merveilleux de la vie, actions et déportemens de la reine Catherine de Médicis*, attributed to Bèze, probably the work of Estienne, and in any case a brilliant piece of writing—first published in 1574. D'Aubigné is also on the Huguenot side against the Queen. Brantôme gives us the extreme of all that could be said in her favour by a partisan of her Court. In De Castelnau, Tavannes, De Bordenaye, and the *Mémoires* of Marguerite de Valois, there is also much to be gathered. The Venetian ambassadors in France at this time, when Venice was still powerful enough to be fearless in judging other nations when she wished, have a feeling of honesty and strength behind them, that gives great value to their impartial judgments, while their artistic sensibility gives a colour and a refinement to their descriptions, very rare in other writings. Finally, a large collection of the actual letters of the Queen-mother afford a source of information that admits of no dispute. Passing over English writers, and omitting the *Life* by Balzac as a brilliant literary paradox, the *Catherine de Médicis, Mère des Rois etc.*, by M. Capefigue, 1856, may be taken as an example of the apologetic school in France, fortunately not a numerous one.

When first Catherine came to the Court to marry the young Dauphin, with her caressing manners and her Spanish etiquette, Diane de Poitiers was pointing out "the shopkeeper's daughter" to the courtiers, and the keen - eyed Venetian ambassador, Marino Giustiniano had already noticed the discontent of the whole nation at the marriage. "Men find," he says, "that the Pope (her uncle) has deceived the King," and the Dauphin himself was no better pleased with the match ; it was not merely as a merchant's daughter,[1] not merely as one to whom

[1] For details of the early life of Catherine see the researches of M. Alberi and M. de Remmont, collected from the archives at Venice. Her descent from the founder of the family is as follows :—

Giovanni de Medici (d. 1428)

Cosmo (Pater Patriae, d. 1464)

Pietro (d. 1472)

Lorenzo il Magnifico (d. 1492)   Julian

Alfonsina, daughter = Pietro the Unfortunate   Pope Clement VII.
of Orsino,
Constable of France

Lorenzo, Duc d'Urbino (d. 1519) = Magdalena,
daughter of Jean de la Tour, Comte
of Boulogne and Auvergne.

Henry II. of France = Catherine de Medici (1519-1589).

It is curious to note that Catherine was distantly related to both her rivals at the French Court—to Marie Stuart through the Duke of Albany, son of James III. and Anne de la Tour, the aunt of Catherine ; to Diane de Poitiers through her father, Jean de Poitiers, whose mother, Jeanne de Boulogne, was an aunt of Magdalena de la Tour.

In connection with Catherine's own children the Pope's remark on leaving her at Marseilles is interesting. "A figlia d' inganno non manca mai la figliuolanza."

deceit and lying were as habitual as breath, that he disliked her, but "as some serpent born of tainted parents in the charnel-houses of Italy." [1]

The strange sight of the foreign wife protected and befriended by the French mistress, is explained by Diana's fear that the throne in default of direct heirs would fall to her enemies ; and when at last a child was born, it was the weak and ill - formed Francis, who died before his time, and bequeathed the civil wars to France ; then came the madman Charles IX., with the blood of St. Bartholomew's Day upon his hands ; then the effeminate Henry, weak and spiteful as he was cowardly, who debased the country to his own degraded level ; and after bearing such a brood, the pale, fat-faced Florentine grew old and battened on the miseries of France. Educated among the faction and intrigue of the Italian Republics, when murder was the habitual solution of a difficulty, with little knowledge of French customs, no prejudices of birth or aristocracy, as incredulous of good as she was superstitious and given over to enchantments,[2] she only saw in France another Florence to be cowed by the old mean methods, and in the factions of Guises and Châtillons

---

[1] She had no children for ten years. This, say her apologists, was more Henry's fault than hers, but the fact remains, and I cannot help seeing more truth in Michelet, than in the untranslatable explanations of Brantôme, Balzac, and the others.

[2] See the traces of her cabalistic figures at Chaumont, her tower "Uraniae Sacrum" at Blois. "The eccentricities of genius," says M. Capefigue.

another quarrel to be settled like the feuds of Medici and Pazzi. Where it was impossible to avail herself of the secrets of Ruggieri, she unhesitatingly made every use which a cynical immorality could suggest of the "escadron volant" that was always at her orders. The statesman whose position saved him from assassination was seldom man enough to resist the temptations of an intrigue ; he was entangled at the critical moment, and his opportunity was lost. Antoine de Navarre and Condé were only two examples among many of the astuteness of the Queen-mother's policy. Jeanne d'Albret's letters from Blois show the disgust and alarm which were aroused in a good woman by contact with this society at Court.[1]

Crushed and humiliated from her very infancy, broken by the contempt of Henry II., at the mercy of his mistress, and eclipsed by the young Queen of Scotland, Catherine seemed to see in the early years of Charles IX.'s reign, her first glimpse of the power she thirsted for, which had almost escaped her in the short life of Francis II.

But the strength of the Guises soon taught her, at Vassy and at Fontainebleau, that her time was not yet.

---

[1] M. Capefigue's explanation is worth hearing. By the sweet influence of the "escadron volant" the soft airs and graces of the Court were to tone down the rough and violent society of the time. "Au milieu des plaisirs des fêtes et du luxe, elle espérait user ces âmes ardentes, ces cœurs de fer et de feu." After this it is only to be expected that we should find that "the Mignons were encouraged to show what a Court ought to be," that "Henry of Navarre was coarse compared with them," and other extraordinary statements.

" She felt their heavy hand upon her neck and bowed her head ; her heart fell back again to the meanness that was natural to it" : she played the good Queen-mother at the Guises' bidding.

" She never leaves the King," writes Giovanni Michiel, who gives some striking details of the life at the French Court. " She keeps the seal which the King uses, which they call cachet. . . . The Queen-mother is very fond of the good things of life ; her habits are irregular and she eats much, but afterwards seeks remedy in strong exercise ; she walks, rides,[1] and is never still ; strangest of all, she has even been seen out hunting. But in spite of all this, her face is always pale and almost of a greenish tinge, and she is very fat." Even the Italian ambassadors cannot find much to praise in their compatriot, though they do their best. " As to the Queen," says another, Michele Suriano, " it is enough to say she is a true Florentine if ever there was one, but it is impossible to deny that she is a woman of great tact and intellectual vigour." Brantôme and Davila agree in this last opinion, which is perhaps the best that can be said of Catherine, for even the feelings of maternity which she shared in common with the brutes were perverted by her superstition and her cruelty, and warped into a preference for the least worthy of her sons, the

[1] " Elle estoit fort bien à cheval et hardie, et s'y tenoit de fort bonne grace, ayant esté la première qui avoit mis la jambe sur l'arçon, d'autant que la grace y estoit bien plus belle et apparoissante que sur la plan-chette."—Brantôme.

miserable Henry, Duc d'Anjou. Her son Charles had only frightened her whenever he attempted to show a will of his own ; for Francis she felt too much contempt for love ; in Henry alone she could see her own nature reflected, womanish and Italian, witty, heartless and corrupted.

It is only necessary to peruse the letters she was perpetually scribbling[1] at this time to be convinced of her true character. Throughout them all is the same undercurrent of commercial vulgarity, of plotting and intrigue, of requests for help for Gondi and Bizago, and the rest of her Italian protégés.

"She does everything a man could do, and yet she is scarcely loved," says Correro again naïvely in the reign of Charles IX. "The Huguenots say that she deceived them by her fair words and her false air of kindliness, while all the time she was plotting their destruction with the Catholic King ; the Catholics, on the other hand, say that if the Queen had not encouraged the Huguenots they would not have gone so far."

"Extremes disgusted her," explains M. Capefigue : "she tried to unite both parties to the King." As a matter of fact she played fast and loose with one after the other, and the only consistent motive in the hand-to-mouth policy of her whole life was her insatiate ambition for her own and for her children's greatness.[2]

---

[1] "Je la vis une fois, pour une après disnée, escrire de sa main vingt pures lettres et longues."—*Brantôme.*

[2] See Martin, *Hist.* ix. 271.

It scarcely needed the terrible picture in Dumas'
Reine Margot, of Catherine ranging like a wolf
among the dead, for us to imagine how she ruined
the diseased and excitable nature of her son Charles,
and drove him slowly mad by hideous plots and
countless thwartings of his feeble attempts at
righteous government. So well recognised had her
character become that the danger of her friendship
was a proverb at the Court.[1] No one could feel safe
with a woman who took such obvious delight in
condemnations and in trials, whose relaxation from
a satiety of festivals was the sight of organised
butcheries, which restored her the energies for
renewed debauchery and dissipation. From the
revels at Blois she moves to the massacres at
Amboise, and completes the round of pleasure with
the fêtes at Chenonceaux : even if her complicity in
the murders of St. Bartholomew were not completely
proved, it would be hard to acquit any one who had
such interest in the death of the Huguenot leaders
as had Catherine, but it was entirely owing to her
evil suggestions that the mind of the unhappy King
was worked up to the pitch of frenzy required to let
loose the wild fanaticism of Paris, that might even
still have been restrained. After the massacre she

---

[1] "Quand elle appelait quelqu'un ' mon amy c'estoit qu'elle l'estimoit
sot ou qu'elle estoit en colère," etc. . . . "Je la vis une fois . . . tout
du long du chemin lire dans un parchemin tout un procès verbal que l'on
avoit fait de Derdois, basque, secretaire favory du Connestable," etc.—
Brantôme.

triumphantly showed the papers of the murdered
Admiral Coligny to Walsingham, Elizabeth's ambassador. "Le voilà votre ami," she cried, "voyez s'il
aimait l'Angleterre."—"Madame," replies the Englishman, "at least he loved France."[1] And as a true
lover of his country, as one of the few real heroes
of that time, Coligny was especially obnoxious to
Catherine ; and France, which still trembled, began
at last to see the truth. "She is accused," says
Giovanni Michiel in 1575, "of every evil that has
desolated the kingdom ; up till this time she was
but little liked, now she is detested." For thirteen
years longer her pale face was at the King's shoulder
whispering the venom of her counsels to his cowardly
heart. In the reign of Henry III. at Blois we shall
meet her again, and there the end comes worthily,
after her son, who had begun his career with the
death of the chief of the Protestants, had ended it
with the murder of the head of the Catholic League.
Her tricks and schemes are over, she is found out at
last, and dies beneath the rooms where Guise was
stabbed to death ; her body, which found but scant
and hasty burial, was left almost forgotten, and
hurried to its tomb from the Church of St. Sauveur.

---

[1] Among many contemporary witnesses see La Noue's testimony to
the worth of Coligny in *Discours Politiques et Militaires*, xxvi. "Trois-
ièmes Troubles," Bâle, 1587, p. 702. "Or, si quelqu'un en ces lamen-
tables guerres a grandement travaillé et du corps et de l'esprit, on peut
dire que c'a esté M. l'Amiral . . . somme, c'était un personnage digne
de restituer un Estat affoibly et corrompue."

CHAPTER XV

AMBOISE

" Carolus Octavus primus me erexit in urbem ;
   Hunc fontem, Hos muros, Hæc mihi templa dedit
Ambosa. "

          BISHOP OF AREZZO TO PIERO DI MEDICI, 1493.

 THE Castle of Amboise stands high above the town, like another Acropolis above a smaller Athens ; it rises upon the only height visible for some distance, and is in a commanding position for holding the level fields of Touraine around it, and securing the passage of the Loire between Tours and Chaumont, which is the next link in the chain that ends at Blois.

The river at this point is divided in two by an island, as is so often the case where the first bridge-builders sought to join the wide banks of the Loire, and on this little spot between the waters Clovis is said to have met Alaric before he overthrew the power of the Visigoths in Aquitaine.

Amboise gains even more from the river than the other châteaux of the Loire. The magnificent round tower that springs from the end of Charles VIII.'s façade completely commands the approaches of the bridge, and the extraordinary effect of lofty masonry, produced by building on the summit of an elevation and carrying the stone courses upwards from the lower ground, is here seen at its best.

Through the white houses of the little town that cluster round the lofty castle, " like crumbs that have fallen from a well-laden table," [1] we passed towards the archway which gives entrance to the castle from behind, though the " drawbridge, which had an invention to let one fall, if not premonished," no longer existed. The moats across which Evelyn passed in 1644, and which are clearly drawn in prints of the sixteenth century,[2] no longer exist. A winding ascent led us into the gardens, which have a special charm of beauty, removed and isolated from the common life below, lifted high in the air on the great rock of the fortress, and surrounded by its towers and terraces. Here we were left to wander for a time when we first arrived, and discovered alone the lovely little chapel of St. Hubert, with an extraordinary carving above the doorway, representing St. Hubert's encounter with the miraculous Stag.

---

[1] Mr. Henry James, *op. cit.* The few chapters on Touraine by this writer are full of picturesque and appreciative touches of the impression which the mere exterior of all these châteaux leaves upon an artistic visitor ; see especially his description of Blois (*A Little Tour in France*).

[2] In the picture of La Renaudie's death, for instance, which will be referred to in subsequent pages.

The building looks very tiny in one corner of this
vast courtyard, but the charming effect of its light
buttresses, rising from below and clinging to the
great outer walls of rock and brickwork until they
end in finely chiselled pinnacles that blossom from
the angles of its roof, is completed by a richness
and care in the workmanship of the interior very
rarely surpassed by any monument of its time ; the
inner surface of its walls is a marvel of beautiful
stone carving fine as lace, and shows up the more as
it is almost the only work of the kind to be seen at
Amboise. The chapel was built [1] by Charles VIII.
after his return from Italy, and was no doubt carved
by the Italian artists who came with him. There is
a strangely grotesque figure of an ape above the
altar, which is mentioned by M. Champfleury
(*Histoire de la Caricature au moyen âge*) as
peculiarly distinctive of that period of Italian taste.
The whole has been restored and strengthened with
the greatest care and success since 1872 by the
architect of M. le Comte de Paris, in whose possession the castle then was, and it is by his care, too,
that the beauty of the great towers, built by Charles
VIII. about the same time, remains in its original

---

[1] Any one who knows Oxford will remember the carving which is
above the entrance gate of Merton ; let him imagine this inserted above
the door of Exeter College Chapel, and the whole raised upon steep
walls many feet into the air, and he will have a faint idea of the chapel
at Amboise, which is on much the same lines (very much reduced, but
in perfect proportion) as the Sainte Chapelle at Paris, with the same
light spire.

condition, stripped of the hideous modern erections which formerly defaced them. Amboise has not always met with such careful treatment ; in 1806 a certain vandal senator, one Roger Ducos, irreparably destroyed a great part of the old buildings to avoid the trouble and expense of keeping them in proper repair ; nor did the war of 1870 spare the place entirely, for when the bridge was blown up, the excessive quantity of powder employed loosened the foundations of several parts of the château, and almost produced incalculable disaster.

Little more than the actual rooms and walls built by Charles VIII., with various modern restorations that were only necessitated from decay and never look incongruous, now remains at Amboise. We shall see more of them as we look closer into the story of the castle, and though of the interior there is absolutely nothing worth inspection left, the outside walls and terraces have a grandeur all their own that compensates for any shortcomings within.

But Amboise has a history before the days of Charles VIII. There was without doubt a Roman camp here, but the traditions of the ubiquitous Cæsar must be received with caution.[1] The so-called

---

[1] The Chronicle written by the monk Jean de Marmoutier in the twelfth century says that Cæsar on his way back from the siege of Bourges was so struck with the strategical position of Amboise that

" Greniers de César," strange, unexplained construc-
tions caverned in the soft rock, are proved to be the
work of a later age by that same indefatigable Abbé
Chevalier to whom we have been already indebted
for so much archæological research. A possible
explanation of them is contained in an old Latin
history of the castle, which goes down to the death
of Stephen of England. According to this,[1] the
Romans had held Amboise from the days of Cæsar
till the reign of Diocletian; the Baugaredi or Bagaudæ
then put them to flight, but let the rest of the inhabitants remain, who, " being afraid to live above
ground, tunnelled beneath it, and made a great colony
of subterranean dwellings in the holes they had dug
out," a custom apparently common in Touraine from
the earliest times, and of which we have already
noticed several instances. The Romans at any rate
left unmistakable traces of their presence ; many of
their architectural remains still exist, and their fort
is spoken of by Sulpicius Severus ; but they can
have built no bridge of stone, for in St. Gregory's

he built a tower upon the rock, and raised upon the whole a great
statue of the god Mars, which fell in a miraculous storm raised by St.
Martin to abolish the emblems of paganism. Touraine is full of the
strangest traditions of Julius Cæsar. The most amusing instance of such
stories I have found is the passport gravely asserted to be authentic
which runs as follows : "Laissez passer le nommé César. (Signé)
Vercingetorix."

[1] "Liber de Compositione Castri Ambaciæ et ipsius Dominorum
Gestis," which is No. 9 in a collection bound together called *Veterum
aliquot Scriptorum qui in Gallia Bibliothecis maxime Benedictorum
latuerant Spicilegium*, tom. x., published in Paris 1671.

time there were only boats available for the crossing of the river.[1]

One more detail occurs in the Latin chronicler which is too attractive to English readers to be omitted, in spite of the suspicions somewhat brutally expressed in a marginal note by some more modern critic. At the time when the Romans had lost all hold upon the province, one Maximus, the captain of the castle, gave his daughter in marriage to the King of Britain, after which it came into possession of King Arthur, who gave it back to the Franks " before he sailed away to conquer Mordred, and was slain in the Isle of Avalon."

But by the time of Clovis, Amboise begins to stand clearly out from the mist of tradition and uncertainty, and in the ninth century the great tower, which had already become a fortress, was in the power of the Counts of Anjou, and in 1016 we hear of the Angevin captain, Pontlevoy, bringing back much plunder from the conquest of Odo of Blois and storing it in the great keep of Amboise.

Not till the fifteenth century did the castle become royal property, when it was confiscated by Charles VII. as a punishment for treacherous dealings with the invading English very similar to the treason discovered at Chenonceaux just before. But beyond strengthening the fortifications of the place this King did little for his new possession.

[1] M. Mabille, *op. cit.* (cap. i.), *Bibl. de l'École des Chartes*, Touraine.

In a few years the castle is overshadowed by
the cruel spectre of Louis XI., whose memory has
already spoilt several charming views for us.   It was
to Amboise that the father of this unfilial prince was
carried from Chinon on his way north, when wearied
out by the annoyance caused by the Dauphin's plots.
The castle had become a royal residence, and soon
after the whole town turns out to meet the new King
with a " moralité que maistre Estienne avait faite
pour jouer ladite joyeuse venue," for Amboise was
already famous for those dramatic performances
always so dear to the French, and particularly to
these citizens, in the old days at any rate.   There is
no trace of such frivolities now in the sleepy little
town.

Then, " wine was given to all comers to drink at
the expense of the town," with a wild hospitality
which told upon the civic treasury somewhat too
heavily ; but they made merry while they could :
Louis XI. was but newly crowned, the whips had not
yet changed to scorpions.   In less than four years
the actors had thrown away their motley, and, clad
in what steel they had, were formed into a civic
guard for the protection of the town.   The Duke of
Burgundy had already begun to show how true he
was to be to the troublesome traditions of his house,
and the word " Peronne " had furnished the latest
jest for Paris, always ready to laugh at a *faux pas*
even of its King.

It was at Amboise that Louis XI. instituted the Order of St. Michael, that was to rival the dignity of the famous Order of the Golden Fleece, and at this time the arms of France were first surrounded with the chain of cockle-shells that held the figure of the Saint conquering Satan.[1] A representation of a meeting of this Order in August 1469 at Amboise occurs in the " Statutes of the Order," dated from Plessis-lez-Tours, which is decorated with miniatures, and preserved at Paris.　·

But in spite of troubles with Burgundy and taxations from the King's council, all brightness was not quite gone from the little town, for more Mystery Plays were occasioned by the birth of the future Charles VIII., and not many years after Louis made his last visit to Amboise to give his son his blessing, whatever that might be worth, before retiring to try to keep out death by lock and key, by moats and man-traps, in his dismal fortress at Plessis-lez-Tours.

During his reign Amboise, both town and castle, suffered from the depression that was general throughout France ; even their Mystery Plays seem to have somewhat flagged. Some three hundred years of jesting at the Pope and the morality of abbeys had begun to weary ; these representations, which had begun by being always of a religious

---

[1] Travellers who have visited Mont St. Michel will agree that the shells from Cancale and that part of the coast quite deserve their proud position in the royal escutcheon.

character, had made a new departure in the *Mistère du Siège d'Orléans*, already quoted ; yet even here there is a whole company of heavenly actors. Before this the author could merely change the words of Scripture in the mouths of secondary personages whose comic interludes produced the only effect that gave success, and were the supreme effort of contemporary dramatic art ; plot there was none, only a multiplicity of variety and scene. Rabelais tells us of Villon's efforts in this direction, and draws several lively pictures of the Comédies and Diableries which followed, for which last the town of Doué was particularly famous.

The " Mystery Plays," properly so called, were of very early origin, and were possibly an attempt to present to all classes a vivid enactment of sacred scenes which had not yet become public property by the agency of the printing press. The story of Daniel, or the parable of the Ten Virgins, became much more of a reality to the common people when actually thrown into life and action before their eyes, than when spelt out with difficulty from a rare manuscript, or misunderstood from the readings of some ecclesiastic in a foreign tongue. The custom thus originated lasted long after the presses of Faust and Gutenberg had popularised literature, sacred and profane, even after the movement of the Reformation had given a French Bible to the nation, and a Marot had produced his metrical version of the Psalms. But it was not from these that the drama of Molière drew its inspiration, nor from what is known as the " profane mystery," a kind of horrible parody upon Biblical subjects, but from the " moralities," the farces, and " soties," which had their origin in the innate dramatic instinct of the French people. The farce of Patelin,[1] for instance, was a very fair reproduction of the manners of the time, and as such it has been already quoted, and indeed so great a hold did these representations gain upon the public mind that we find such a piece as the *Farce du Pasté et de la Tarte* retaining its popularity until the days of Louis XIV., when Molière's company took the place of the Comédiens de l'Hôtel de Bourgogne. These last " Comédiens " were a survival of the old " Confrèrie de la Passion," a society of actors who had almost superseded the old " Basoche " and the " Enfants sans Souci," by an audacious mixture of the old and established Scriptural subjects with grotesque or obscene incidents which appealed to the grossness of the time, while it reflected the chaotic nature of the religious sympathies and beliefs of men in the thick darkness of the Middle Ages. There is in them the same ghastly mockery of holiness which disgusts us chiefly in the character of Louis XI.,

[1] The farce of Patelin was very celebrated in the sixteenth century. It was composed between 1467 and 1470. For a criticism and analysis of it see Estienne Pasquier, *Recherches*, viii. 59, p. 780 (ed. 1621).

as it will sicken us later on in Henry III. The hideous cloak of superstition and idolatry which Louis called religion, still more perhaps the heartless cruelty of the man in private as well as in public relations with his fellow-man, all this remained far too clear for us to be long doubtful about the sincerity of the joy of Amboise when the old cry was heard again, " Le Roi est mort, vive le roi."

For some time the Dauphin had been living at Amboise in idleness and seclusion ; but the accounts of his father's neglect are not to be too hastily believed. Louis has quite enough to answer for without this being laid to his charge unnecessarily, and the testimony of Commines on the point is to be received with caution. The scene at the castle in September 1482, when Louis, just returned from a pilgrimage to Saint Claude, and feeling that his end was near, solemnly invested his son with the royal authority, would seem to show that his neglect of Charles has been somewhat exaggerated ; but there is other evidence, too : the letters of the King to Bourré, who had charge of the Prince, are not those of a careless and indifferent father, nor would a man whose ideas of classical education were limited by the sentence " Qui nescit dissimulare nescit regnare " so highly reward Étienne de Vesc, the other tutor. Such a maxim was at any rate not the one by which the new King guided his policy ; nor was his reading, even before he came to the throne, limited to the

romances of chivalry by which his mother's notions
of literature were bounded. The *Grandes Chroniques
de France* and the *Rosier des Guerres* of Pierre
Choinet were in his hands soon after 1482, and
this ignorant prince, who was supposed to have been
suppressed for fear of opposition to his father's
power, astonishes Europe by an invasion of Italy
as soon as the disturbances of his own nobles within
the kingdom had been quelled.

It is well known, too, that his was a mind which
developed slowly and would bear but little pressure.
Claude de Seyssel and Commines give the wrong
reason for the education prescribed for Charles by
his father. From Nicole Gilles we find what is far
nearer the truth, that the life of the heir to the
throne was rightly considered to be of more importance than the acuteness of his intellect, and that his
strength of body was encouraged in preference to
the risk of enfeebling a naturally weak constitution
by the enforcement of displeasing studies. "Sa
mauvaise nourriture," as Commines calls it, "n'en-
dommagea en rien son généreux naturel brave
courage qui était né avec lui," and when he was
strong enough to learn he had the will to study.
The number of classical books which he brought
back from Italy would alone prove that his tastes in
this direction had not been neglected ; and though
inevitably much was wanting in his general education, yet the sound advice and firm policy of the

Regent, Anne de Beaujeu, did much to steer him safely through the first troubled years of the reign that he began when still a child.

The young King's return from his campaign in Italy, unpleasant enough in its inevitable ill-success, was still further saddened by the death of his son at three years of age, " bel enfant," says Commines, " et audacieux en parole ; et ne craignant point les choses que les autres enfants ont accoutumé de craindre." This boy was buried with his brother in the Church of St. Martin at Tours, and their tomb is still one of the most beautiful ornaments of the cathedral to which it was removed after the destruction of the older church.

The two great towers of Amboise with the inclined planes of brickwork, which wind upwards in the midst instead of staircases, were the result of the work which Charles set on foot as a distraction to his grief. These strange ascents had been partially restored by the Comte de Paris, the present owner of Amboise, before his exile stopped the work of repairing the château, and it is still possible to imagine the " charrettes, mullets, et litières," of which Du Bellay speaks, mounting from the low ground to the chambers above, or the Emperor Charles V., in later years, riding up with his royal host, Francis I., always fond of display, amid such a blaze of flambeaux " that a man might see as clearly as at mid-day."

CHARLES ORLANDO, ELDEST SON OF CHARLES VIII., from the original in the possession of M. Bligny, Paris, painted on wood at the end of the fifteenth century, artist unknown, probably Jean Perréal.

Reproduced by permission of M. Péricat, Tours.

These great towers and the exquisite little chapel were the work of the "excellent sculptors and artists from Naples" who, as Commines tells us, were brought back with the spoils of the Italian wars ; for the young King "never thought of death" but only of collecting round him "all the beautiful things which he had seen and which had given him pleasure, from France or Italy or Flanders ;"[1] but death came upon him suddenly. At the end of a garden walk, fringed with a mossy grove of limes that rises from the river bank, is the little doorway through which Charles VIII. was passing when he hit his head, never a very strong one, against the low stone arch, and died a few hours afterwards. The castle had been fortified before his time ; he left it beautiful as well, and the traces of his work are those which are most striking at the present day.[2]

[1] In October and November 1493 he shows off the new buildings with much pride to the Italian ambassadors. See Desjardins, *Négot. Diplom. de la F. avec la Toscane*, i. 340.

[2] Baron de Cosson has been kind enough to send me a list of the arms and armour in the Château of Amboise at 1499. It will be noticed that the ownership of King Arthur is traceable in the entry referring to Lancelot's sword. "Une dague en manchée de licorne la poignée de cristalin nommée la dague Saint-Charlemagne. Une espée en manchée de fer, garnie en façon de clef nommée l'espée de Lancelot du Lac, et dit-on qu'elle est fée. Une espée d'armes garnie de fouet blanc et au pommeau une Nostre Dame d'un costé et un souleil de l'autre, nommée l'espée du Roy Charles VII., appellée la bien-aimée. Une espée d'armes, la poignée couverte de fouet blanc et au pommeau a une Nostre Dame d'un costé et un S. Michel de l'autre, nommée l'espée du Roy de France qui fist armes contre un géan à Paris et le conquist." Various other swords are mentioned, such as the Papal one given with the arms of Pope Calixtus ; the war-sword of Charles VIII. ;

The new reign began with the disgraceful process of divorce against the first wife of the King, Jeanne de France ; in the Church of St. Denys it was confirmed publicly, and the papal sanction read. The indignation which must have been felt pretty generally throughout France was particularly outspoken in Amboise, where the prelates and theologians of the Court were pointed out in the streets as the " Herods and Pilates " of their time.

It may have been as much a feeling of shame as a movement prompted by more delicate associations, which prevented Louis from entering the town with Anne de Bretagne when she made her second entry as Queen of France. Amboise was, as usual, ready with its Mystery Play to welcome the new Queen— this time a history of Julius Cæsar—but the demonstration of loyal and dramatic fervour was suppressed.

a sword given by the King of Scotland to Louis XI. when he married Madame la Dauphine ; the sword of Louis XI., "nommée la belle espée du Roy Louis qu'il avoit à la conqueste qu'il fist premier sur les Suysses, nommée Estrefuse"; a sword "nommée l'espée de Philippe le Bel"; another "nommée l'espée du Roy Jehan"; with others belonging to Louis XI. and Charles VIII. The sword called "La Victoire" seems to have been made for Charles VI. in 1383 (see V. Gay, *Glossaire Archéologique*, Paris, 1887, p. 686). Amongst the armour was, "Une brigandine de Tallebot couverte de veloux noir tout usée, et sa salade noire couverte d'un houx de broderie fait sur veloux, tout usée"; also, "Harnoys de la pucelle, garny de garde-bras, d'une paire de mitons, et d'un abillement de teste où il y a ung gorgeray de maille, le bort doré, le dedans garny de satin cramoisy, doublé de mesme." There was besides "une hache à une main qui fut au Roy Saint Loys" (see V. Gay, p. 65).

At this time the Maréchal de Gié, whom we have met before, begins to take a prominent position. He had accompanied the King on the first expedition to Italy, and after his return had been moved, by a sudden accident to Louis, to think of the marriage of his daughter Claude. Unfortunately Anne de Bretagne, never a great friend to the Maréchal, had thought about it too, and hostilities began between them, on the Queen's side " une guerre de coups d'épingle," on the Maréchal's nothing save a profound and apparent contempt.[1] De Gié was now given the care of Louise de Savoie, Comtesse d'Angoulême, and her children, with a small force of men-at-arms in the Castle of Amboise, and by his command in Angers, and his connections in Saumur and Tours, he was practically master of the Loire—a fact which was peculiarly galling to the Queen, for by way of trying, like a true Breton, to guarantee her eventual independence, she was in the habit of sending jewels and other valuables down the river to safe-keeping at Nantes ; but this, though it was to appear again later on, was not the chief grievance of which the Queen complained, for De Gié had a far higher task : he was holding the future Francis I. against all other possible heirs whom Anne de Bretagne might produce by marrying her daughter to a foreign prince, and his position was made all the more

---

[1] See *Procédures Politiques du règne de Louis XII.*, M. de Maulde, École des Chartes.

difficult by the narrow and suspicious nature of
Louise de Savoie.

But between De Gié and D'Amboise was now
divided the chief power in the kingdom, and he soon
began definite negotiations for the marriage of Francis
with the Princess Claude. Anne de Bretagne, as we
have seen, was actually desirous of giving her daughter
to the boy who was to become Charles V., and the
value of De Gié's authority in French politics may
be estimated by this fact alone of spirited opposition
to so grave an error.

Nor were his energies exhausted upon this one
struggle. He found time to send opportune help to
the French army that was struggling in Italy, and,
though fifty-two years of age, to marry Marguerite
d'Armagnac and obtain the title of Duc de Nemours.
It was owing to his exertions, too, that a National
Infantry, some twenty thousand strong, was raised, and
when the Cardinal returned in all the disappointment of his lost opportunities at Rome, De Gié's position of confident authority in France added one more
sting to the annoyance of his own failures in Italy.

But the Maréchal's well-merited good fortune did
not last. His son's wife and his own died within a
short interval, and in January 1504 the King fell suddenly very ill, and was sent to Blois to recover in the
healing influence of his natal air, as Francis was sent
later on to Cognac, in accordance with a medical
superstition for long prevalent in France.

It now became more than ever important to urge on the marriage of Francis and the princess, and in the opposition that ensued Cardinal d'Amboise joined the Queen against De Gié and resolved upon his fall, making various accusations as to his unwarrantable interference with the Queen's movements ; indeed, just at this time the Maréchal had seized two boats laden with her furniture and jewels between Saumur and Nantes, which were on their way westwards to provide a comfortable provision for the widowhood which then seemed near at hand. Anne was furious, and her anger was increased by the betrothal of Francis. She at once instituted proceedings against De Gié, but his character and probity were too well known for her to succeed. But the Queen would not rest without her vengeance, got up another trial, and condemned him at the Court of Toulouse, while D'Amboise looked on, and "let justice take its course."

De Gié, banished from the Court and heavily fined, went into an honourable retirement at his Château of Verger, which recalled in many details the home at Blois of the King he had served so well. The process which the Queen instituted against him proved his justification for all time, and purified his memory for ever from the calumnies of the Court. He was too honest and too straightforward for those with whom he had to come in contact, and, like Semblançay afterwards, he had to pay the penalty for his integrity. He reorganised the army, established a sound defence on the frontiers, and invariably opposed the foreign expeditions which wasted to so little purpose the resources of the kingdom ; it is in this that his greatness consists, for perhaps he was alone of his time in realising that the strength of France lay in her natural boundaries, and alone in devoting his energies to the unity and solidification of his country.

In 1507, at the engagement of the Princess Claude to Francis, then the probable heir to the throne, the enthusiastic citizens of Amboise would not be denied their usual tribute of congratulation, and the *Mystère de la Passion* was presented with so much magnificence that the town accounts were in hopeless confusion for a long while afterwards.

Francis I., whose long nose and slumbrous eye look down from the walls of so many châteaux of Touraine, has been at Amboise for some time. The reader has already been introduced to him in later life, and to his sister, the learned Marguerite, who in 1501, at the age of nine, was watching her brother, two years younger than herself, playing with little Fleurange, who had just made his youthful début at Blois, and had been sent on by the King to keep the young duke company. They played a rough kind of tennis in the level spaces of the garden, using a racquet weighted with lead to give more force to their blows, or shot with bows and arrows at a white

mark fixed to a door, or, as the prince's strength
grew with his age, a new game is introduced from
Italy, played with enormous hollow balls that were
struck with a queer instrument of metal covered
with felt and tied on the arm from wrist to elbow
with leathern straps ; and now, finding that four
make a better game than two, Francis takes young
Anne de Montmorency to try conclusions with Brion
Chabot, who is partner to Robert de la Marche.

Two of the players were to turn their mimic
rivalry into grim earnest later on, and all were to
be famous ; perhaps they felt that even now, for
when the game is over, the little snub nose of " Le
Camus " may be seen in close proximity to the
lengthy face of Francis, asking the duke to make
him Constable some day, when he shall have come
into his kingdom ; while Chabot, not to be left
behind, begs to be Admiral of France in that
glorious future when they shall help together to
regenerate the world. Both had their wish, and
Montmorency, the Constable, lived sternly through
the next four reigns, to die fighting in 1567 at the
battle of St. Denis.

With these boys there are others, too, who shall
be famous in their deaths. Gaston de Foix, who died
so young at Ravenna ; Bonnivet, who was to fall in
love with the fair sister of his playmate and die upon
the field of Pavia, where Fleurange, too, was taken
prisoner, and used his hours of solitude to write his

Mémoires. And watching her son with eyes as eager as her daughter's, and even more ambitious, is Louise de Savoie, whose short journal, full of this idolised son, gives us many details of his life at Amboise.

In January 1501 she writes : " About two in the afternoon my king, my lord, my Cæsar, and my son, was run away with across the fields near Amboise by a pony which the Maréchal de Gié had given him ; the danger was so great that those present considered it past remedy. Nevertheless God, the protector of widow women and the defence of orphans, foreseeing the future, would not abandon me, knowing that had ill fortune robbed me suddenly of my love I should have been too unhappy."

This journal, which is the barest chronicle of facts and dates, the narrow record of a mean character, never rises into pretentious diction but when speaking of this boy on whom her whole soul rested. The strong young prince was soon to leave the castle, where his impetuous nature had often frightened others besides his anxious mother. One day he let a wild boar loose within the court, which rushed madly at the flying servants, and finally made for the great staircase, where Francis was waiting and killed it with his dagger.

Soon after, Louise writes : " Mon fils partit d'Amboise pour être homme de cour et me laissa toute seule "—there is all a mother's pathos in these short words ; but the diary still contains references

DOOR OF CHAPEL AT THE CHÂTEAU OF AMBOISE. The smaller carving represents St.
Hubert meeting the miraculous Stag; above are the statues of Louis XII. and Anne
de Bretagne.

to his visits to the castle; once when on his way to
Guienne against the Spaniards in 1512, and three
years later when he rides over from Chaumont with
a thorn in his leg, "from which," writes his mother,
"he had much pain, and I too."

Then after some terrible sidelights upon the jealousy
between the Savoyard and the Breton woman, comes
"the triumphant entry" of the death of Louis XII.
without male issue, and the coronation of her beloved
Francis. Between the births of his daughters, Louise
and Charlotte, at Amboise, the tidings of Marignano
came to Louise. "The fight began," she writes, "at
five in the afternoon and lasted all the night; that
very day (13th September 1515) I left Amboise to
go on foot to Notre Dame de Fontaines, to recommend to her him whom I love more than myself,
my glorious son and my victorious Cæsar, who has
subdued the Helvetians." On the same day there
was seen in Flanders a great comet shaped like a
lance; the beginning of the reign of Francis was
crowned with military glory; we have already seen
how it ended.

Within the shadow of the lime trees on the
terraced garden of Amboise is a small bust of
Leonardo da Vinci, for it was near here that he
died. His remains are laid in the beautiful chapel
at the corner of the castle court, and the romantic
story of his last moments at Fontainebleau becomes
the sad reality of a tombstone covering ashes mostly

unknown and certainly indistinguishable ; " amongst
which," as the epitaph painfully records, " are supposed to be the remains of Leonardo da Vinci." He
had been brought to Paris a weak old man of sixty-
five, by Francis, in pursuance of a certain fixed artistic
policy, to which it may be noticed this forgotten and
uncertain grave does but little credit.

To Francis I., rightly or wrongly, is given the glory
of having naturalised in France the arts of Italy ; to
him is due the architecture built for ease and charm
which turned the fortress into a beautiful habitation,
which changed Chambord from a feudal stronghold to
a country seat, and which left its traces at Amboise, as
it did at Chaumont and at Blois.   He found in France
the highest and most beautiful expression of the work
of " the great unnamed race of master-masons ; " he
found the traditions of a national school of painting,
the work of Fouquet and the Clouets, but for these
he cared not ; [1] for him the only schools were those of
Rome and Florence, and though by encouraging their
imitation he weakened the vital sincerity of French

---

[1] For an account of Fouquet, see chapter on the Dukes of Orleans.
Jehan Clouet, called Janet, was Court painter to Francis I. after 1518,
and died in 1540. His painting is notable for its simplicity and delicacy.
His best known works are the equestrian portrait of Francis (on parch-
ment) in the Uffizi, and the half-length on panel at Versailles. There
is also a portrait of the Princess Marguerite in the Royal Institution by
him, though it is usually attributed to Holbein, with whom the school
of the Clouets was contemporary.   There are other fine examples of
their work at Hampton Court, notably the Dauphin Francis. The most
famous of the family, François Clouet, was born at Tours, and the castles
on the Loire contain several examples of his work.

art, yet from his first exercise of royal power the consistency always somewhat lacking in his politics was shown clearly and firmly in his taste for art.

Only the pupils of the other great masters were to be had from Italy; so Giovanni Battista Rosso (known in France as Maître le Roux), who had studied under Michael Angelo, came to Paris for a sufficient inducement. The Raphaelesque figures of Francesco Primaticcio soon presented a contrast to Le Roux's more vigorous handling, and the quarrel between the two artists, which only ended in Rosso's suicide, was still more embittered by the arrival of the masterly and impudent Benvenuto Cellini, whose extraordinary autobiography gives many piquant details of his stay in France.

But while the King was employing his Italians upon Fontainebleau, Jean Bullant was already at work, who built Ecouen for the Constable,[1] and Goujon, who was to carve the Diane Chasseresse for Anet. The truly original art of these men, some of whom had need of help, some of whom, like Lescot, the Sieur de Clagny, were strong enough to

---

[1] Jean Bullant was the last of the old master-masons and the first of the great architects of France. Of the palace he began in Paris for Catherine de Medicis nothing is left but a large Doric column, now attached to the modern Halle aux Blés. The Queen used to climb up its staircase to consult the stars. With Bullant at Ecouen was Goujon, who began life as a simple mason under Maître Quesnel, and began a long friendship with Pierre Lescot by working with him at the Rood Screen of St. Germain l'Auxerrois. His best works are the Diane Chasseresse, and the statues of the Hôtel Carnavalet.

stand alone, went on its own way untouched by the foreign influences which Francis brought from Italy, or only using the best of the ideas which the foreign workmen brought them.

The whole question of the position of Francis in the movement of the Renaissance is far beyond the scope of these chapters, but three things at least seemed clear to us as we stood by the tomb of Leonardo at Amboise—that there was a strong national school of sculpture, of painting, and of architecture in France that deserved more encouragement from the French King than it obtained ; that " the first pure dream" of art from Italy by which the spirits of this older school were touched, was worth far more both to the nation and to the interests of art than the decadence of the Italy which Francis brought to Paris ; and finally, that if the King so far neglected the greatest of all those whom he invited to his Court, the most accomplished and most varied intellect the world has ever seen, he can have had but little true appreciation of the foreign talent for whose sake he neglected the vigorous schools of art and industry at home.

CHAPTER XVI

AMBOISE—THE CONSPIRACY

" Ne presche plus en France une Évangile armée,
Un Christ empistolé, tout noirci de fumée,
Protant un morion en teste, et dans sa main
Un large coutelas rouge de sang humain. "

DIANE DE POITIERS does not seem to have cared much for Amboise, so the reign of Henry II. does not come into its story, but with the boy who followed Henry to the throne begins the most terrible scene in the history of the castle.

WEATHERCOCK WITH THE ROYAL ARMS, from the Château of Amboise.

In November 1559, Marie Stuart was riding into Amboise with her young husband, Francis II., barely fifteen years of age, beneath the bright crisp sunshine of a winter in Touraine, through gaily-decorated streets filled with a crowd of men and women cheering the new King and his northern bride. Five months afterwards Marie Stuart rode through the same

streets again, with none to watch her but armed
men, the doors and windows of the houses closed,
and only here and there a gibbet or a corpse by way
of decoration. For the little town had suddenly
become the centre of a widespread movement —
a movement which had begun many years ago, and
gradually gathered force almost unseen and un-
appreciated by the Court, until at last it broke
suddenly and terribly into view with the conspiracy
of Amboise.

The strangely new doctrines of Calvin had begun
to penetrate Touraine soon after Francis I. had
brought the Italian Renaissance into France, and
the queer cave dwellings in the rocks of St. Georges
and Rochecorbon already concealed hermits with
tendencies too revolutionary and unorthodox to be
sheltered in ordinary resting-places. But the full
consequences of the spread of the new doctrines did
not become apparent until later, and it was not until
the accession of a mere child to the throne that
the feeling to which those doctrines had given rise
joined itself to a more definite political grievance,
and became the expression of an actual party in the
kingdom.

At the death of Henry II. the influence of the
Guises became paramount at Court, and it was the
policy of Catherine to join their party and to secure
the additional support of the Constable Montmorency,
whose nephews, Admiral Coligny and his brother

D'Andelot, were in the opposition with the Bourbon princes, Antoine, King of Navarre, the Prince of Condé, and the Cardinal de Bourbon. It was therefore necessary, if the Guises were to have a free hand, that the ground should be first cleared, and Catherine was persuaded to send the Bourbon princes and their following away from Court. At the same time began fresh religious persecutions, with a vigour encouraged by the promises which the Cardinal de Guise had made to his foreign allies, to root out once and for all the troublesome heresy from France. Already the persecutions had developed into a reign of terror which began with half-drunken slaughters in the Rue Marais and lasted all the winter, and the iniquitous trial of Du Bourg at length frightened the Huguenots into writing for help to the Bourbons ; the opposition in politics was thus brought into relations with the opposition in religion, and gained in strength from its new ally.

Catherine had characteristically promised help to the Huguenots, without the faintest intention of giving any assistance, and had even gone so far as to tell Coligny that she would see and listen to a clergyman of the reformed religion whom he would send her. As a matter of fact she was completely in the power of the Guises, and it was against this power, which was already felt and resented in wider circles than those immediately about the Court, that the first blow was to be aimed, for the greatest

indignation had been aroused throughout the
kingdom by their flat refusal to summon the States-
General.

Meanwhile the King suddenly grew weaker than
ever, and was ordered by his physicians to spend the
winter and spring at Blois, where terrible rumours
began to be circulated as to the methods to be employed for his recovery.[1] During his illness occurred
the mysterious murder of the President, Antoine
Minard, in Paris. He was a partisan of the Guises,
and they at once made swift reprisals. Du Bourg
was condemned and burnt at St. Jean en Grève.[2]
The Huguenots could wait no longer, and they
found themselves irreparably joined to the great
party of the " Discontented," which now contained
three main elements, — the first, imbued with an
honest zeal for their religion, and with a thoroughly
sincere devotion to their country and their King ;
the second, mainly composed of the more ambitious
spirits eager for some change from the present
miserable state of affairs ; the third, eager for
vengeance on the Guises, both for public and for
private reasons.

Moved by these various feelings the Huguenot

---

[1] He was supposed, absolutely without foundation, to be desirous of
bathing in the blood of infants to remove the blotches on his skin. See
the *Mémoires* of Louis Regnier de la Planche, from whom in the main
the following account of the conspiracy is taken, in combination with
the testimony of Vieilleville and of De Castelnau.

[2] See Bib. Nat. Estampes, *Hist. de Fr.* reg. Q. b. 19.

party went for counsel to their natural leaders, the Princes of the Blood, " qui sont nés en tel cas légitimes magistrats," and their cause was at once taken up by Louis de Bourbon, Prince of Condé. The gist of their demands was, to oust the usurpers, to get hold of the persons of François, Duc de Guise, and of his brother Charles, the Cardinal, and then to try them for their many sins before the States-General, which would be immediately summoned.

The difficulty lay in the first move ; but a man was forthcoming at the crisis, " a certain gentleman from Perigord, Godefroy de Barry, Seigneur de la Renaudie," who at once proffered his services, and bent so keenly to his task that in a few weeks a great assembly of nobles was being secretly held at Nantes to discuss the plan of action. All treasonable attempts against the King himself were from the first distinctly repudiated. The first resolution of the assembly ran as follows : " Protestation faite par *le chef* et tous ceux du conseil, de n'attenter aucune chose contre la majesté du roi, princes du sang, ni État légitime du royaume."

" Le chef" was of course Condé, and his name of " chef muet " had a distinct meaning in the plan of the conspiracy : to his party he was a " leader," to the Court he was " dumb " ; and it was with the distinct approval of his party that he went into Amboise later on, to give them assistance from within, when it should be needed, without arousing the suspicion

of the Guises.   Neither he nor his friends imagined
the terrible position in which he was to be placed.

The council at Nantes further resolved that on
the 10th of March (1560) the Guises should be
seized at Blois.   De Castelnau was given command
of the Gascons, and captains were similarly appointed
for the levies that were to come from every province.[1]

The whole project was very properly condemned
by the far-seeing ministers of Geneva as being impossible without treasonable practices. The King, if he
was to be taken out of the power of the Guises, must
presumably be handed over to Condé ; but the re-
monstrance came too late.   The movement went on
and grew in strength, people came together with the
idea of presenting their grievances to the King, in all
confidence marching without much mystery and by
every road to the Loire, many without knowing of
the plot of La Renaudie or ever having heard his
name : this is most clearly seen from the fact that
his death did not stop the others gathering from all
round, intent on getting audience from the King in
spite of the hated Guises, and the swift executions
did not stay the tide that kept pouring in from the
woods only to be mercilessly killed.

While making his preparations in Paris La Renaudie lodged with one Des Avenelles, who was supposed
to be a Huguenot, but who disclosed as much as he

---

[1] For a list of the Captains and Provinces in the plan of the Conspiracy, see Mezeray, iii. 18 (fol. 1685).

could discover of the whole affair to the secretaries of Duke Francis and the Cardinal. The Guises were thunderstruck at the extent of the conspiracy; they had always suspected the Châtillons, but they could not understand this widespread movement. Their ally, the King of Spain, was far better informed. Coligny, D'Andelot, and Condé had all been in communication with Elizabeth, and Anabaptists, Calvinists, and Huguenots in England, in Switzerland, and in Germany, were all vaguely conscious that some attempt was to be made.

In fear for the King's safety—for they realised as well as their opponents the importance of the royal person—they hurriedly moved the Court from Blois to what was considered the far safer fortress of Amboise, where, as a matter of fact, the castle was almost without troops or stores, where the town was full of Protestants, and Tours hard by was hostile or indifferent. With three hundred resolute men La Renaudie might have succeeded yet, but he was fettered by advices from Nantes, fatally hindered by the number of his accomplices, and ended by waiting too long for the decisive stroke.

The Guises had at any rate the merit of swiftly realising the emergency of the situation. They sent out messengers in every direction calling for help; they did their utmost to arouse popular hatred against the Huguenots by numberless accusations fabricated with the utmost disregard for truth;

finally, they tried to get hold of the chiefs of the conspiracy.

The Admiral and his brother came immediately they were summoned, and the Guises got nothing but very plain speaking from Coligny. " They were disgusted," said he, " that the affairs of the State should be wholly managed by persons whom men considered to be foreigners ; what was needed was a good edict in clear, significant, and unambiguous terms that both parties should be bound to keep."

Condé came in too; not seduced this time by the attractions of the "escadron volant," though Catherine doubtless put him down among her many victims, but of his own free will, to brave out the Guises and call an assembly of the States-General when the plot was over.

The day for the attempt had been fixed afresh for the 16th of March. Young Ferrières was to go first to the castle with some hundred men, who were to be concealed hard by, La Renaudie and De Castelnau would follow with the rest from Noizay, which was the new headquarters now the Court had moved ; a signal would be given from the roof of the castle that all was going well within, and then " le chef muet " was to speak.

But most unfortunately a certain Captain Lignières had broken his oath and betrayed all to Catherine de Medicis. The Guises then roused the country on the plea of an attack against the King's safety,

and affairs began to come to a crisis. Soon afterwards the Comte de Lancerre, with a few of the
garrison from Amboise, met De Castelnau in the
woods and attempted to arrest him, but astonished
at the numbers who suddenly appeared to his
assistance, they retired precipitately and rushed
back to Amboise shouting, "Treason, help, in the
King's name!" No one looked out except a baker,
who shut his door again immediately, and De
Castelnau might have easily secured the town by
a sudden attack. The Court was alarmed by the
discouraging news of thirty captains and five
hundred cavalry waiting with a good company
of men-at-arms at Noizay, and Vieilleville was
asked to represent to them the baseness of their
conduct, and offer a free pass to the presence
of the King.

Nothing would do, however, but the word of
a prince of the blood, so the Duc de Nemours
appeared, and "having sworn on the faith of a
prince, on his honour, and on the damnation of
his soul, and having further signed with his own
hand his name, Jacques de Savoie," he led De
Castelnau and the Huguenot deputies into the
castle, "all considering it a great honour and advantage to have thus free access to the King."

The inevitable result followed. They were seized,
thrown into prison, and "tormented with hellish
cruelty." Chancellor Olivier was forced to explain

the nature of a royal promise, and the executions began, much to the disgust of the Duc de Nemours, whose word had so cynically been disregarded. Vieilleville, well pleased to be out of so discreditable an affair, was sent to Orleans.

Meanwhile La Renaudie, hearing of the danger from a distance, sent help ; his men were all seized by the Guises' cavalry. By bands of tens, fifteens, and twenties they were tied to the horses' tails and dragged in to death ; the better-dressed were killed at once, stripped, and left dead in the ditches. The Guises felt that they were not safe yet, and they resolved to play desperately " for double or quits." But on the 18th they began to feel more assured, for La Renaudie himself, whose bravery deserved a better fate, was shot by a servant of the Baron de Pardeillan, whom he had killed at the same moment in a chance encounter in the woods. His body was carried to the town and hung upon the bridge with a placard stuck upon the neck.

But the Guises still chafed at the sight of their enemies within the castle. They strove to make out that the conspiracy was not against themselves at all, but that their name was used merely as a pretext to abolish monarchy, to reduce France to a republic of Cantons, to kill off the nobility and establish Communism. To try and prove this they made fruitless efforts to collect evidence of treason from Navarre, or from La Bigne, the servant of La Renaudie ; but they could elicit no more than the truth, "that no treason against the King was meant." Their efforts succeeded better with the lower classes : all the scoundrels of the neighbourhood rallied to the powerful Guises. Some two thousand idlers, mule-teers, grooms, carters, lackeys, ruffians of all kinds, flocked to the rich plunder of arms and clothing like kites upon the carrion : many peaceable merchants were robbed of their clothing and all that they possessed, and murdered as heretics if they offered to resist.

The slaughter of the wretched Huguenots went on bravely throughout all the forest paths, and "many others," says De Castelnau, "were taken and hanged to serve as a precedent in so strange a case ; a certain number, too, were strung up to the battlements of the castle to astonish the rest." For a month this went on, till every cut-throat in the Guises' pay had made his fortune, for the country swarmed with men who waited to be killed, or citizens like those of Toulouse who refused to move before they had spoken with the King, and were only cured of their importunity by being hanged from the castle windows.

The young King tried to mitigate the severity of the Guises, exclaiming in horror "at the punishment of so many of my poor subjects," but it was no use. Stronger heads than his had given way in the crisis. The miserable Chancellor Olivier, forced against his

will to connive at all this blood-shedding, shrieked
aloud as he saw the dripping hands of one of
the Protestant noblemen kneeling at the block in
fervent prayer.   He was carried to his bed mortally
sick, where the Cardinal de Guise visited him to
check this strange weakness of an officer of the
Court.   " Ha ! mauldit Cardinal," cried Olivier, " tu
te dampnes et nous fais aussi tous damnez."—" My
son," said the prelate, " resist the Evil One."—" So
he has come at last ! " cried the other with a hideous
laugh, as he turned his back upon De Guise and
died.

The scene at the castle at this time was a terrible
one.   The passages and courts were thronged with
men and women crying for justice or for mercy ;
whole families were to be seen in despair at the
approaching death of a father or a husband ; but no
energy, no bribery, no intercession availed to stay
the vengeance of the Guises ; if their cruelty was
unparalleled, their precautions were infinite as well.
The most brilliant example of their stage manage-
ment was yet to come.

Beneath the walls of the castle, in full view of
that iron balcony whose bars rusted blood-red still
guard the windows looking down upon the Loire,
the scaffolds had been raised with great magni-   ,
ficence : all round the square in which they stood
were lines of planked seats rising in tiers from the
ground, and filled with an expectant crowd ; the

THE CHÂTEAU OF AMBOISE FROM THE LOIRE,

showing the gallery from which the Court watched the execution of the Huguenots ; on the left is the Round Tower of Charles VIII.

night before, thousands of people had slept in the fields around the town to avoid being late for the sight of the morrow, the very roofs were black with sightseers, and a merry barter was carried on, by the fortunate owners of houses looking out upon the square, for spaces at the windows which gave a good view of the block and the scaffold draped in black.

After mass in the castle and the various churches of the town, the lines of the Scottish guard, who had been holding the ground since daybreak, were broken by the first of the Huguenot nobles reserved for execution before the royal presence. All those who could walked bravely forward, speaking little save to refuse the help of the Catholic monks who pressed the hated faith upon them to the last ; many, with faces white and drawn and reddening bandages about their feet, were helped by their friends towards the place of execution ; these were they who had been tortured beforehand in the dungeons of Amboise.

The whispers of the crowd were suddenly hushed, for from the mouths of all the prisoners rose the words of the Psalm, which Clement Marot had not long ago translated, " God be merciful unto us and bless us ; and show us the light of His countenance," [1] and as

---

[1] " Dieu nous soit doux et favorable
Nous bénissant par sa bonté,
Et de son visage adorable
Nous fasse luire la clarté.

the crowd heard the last notes die away and followed
the singers' eyes with theirs, they saw a quick movement of all the prisoners' heads ; the Prince of Condé
had appeared upon the gallery above between the
young Queen, Marie Stuart, and the Duke of Orleans,
and all the gentlemen, his followers who were about
to die, had saluted the prince, their "chef muet." He
was brave enough to give them the last satisfaction
of a dangerous farewell.

The Court had just left the dining-hall, and had
been all led out, men, women and children, by the
Duke of Guise to see this last and finest execution
of the rebels. The ladies shuddered at first, but
Catherine de Medicis was there to show them the
conduct proper to a loyal friend of the little trembling
King, who would have turned his head away but did
not dare. Behind the two Queens stood the Papal
Nuncio, below was the Lieutenant-General, with the
marshals and their suite on horseback. The whole
Court was there, as ready, apparently, for the executions of Amboise as they had been for the fêtes
just finished in the hall at Blois. But not all, we

> " Dieu, tu nous as mis à l'épreuve
>   Et tu nous as examinés,
>   Comme l'argent que l'on éprouve
>   Par le feu tu nous as affinés.

> " Tu nous as fait entrer et joindre
>   Aux pièges de nos ennemis,
>   Tu nous as fait les reins astreindre
>   Des filets où tu nous as mis."

may at least believe, were there of their own will : if it be too true that the young Marie Stuart stood and watched this horrible execution, she was at least no more willing to look on than was the Prince of Condé ; both were forced by the iron will of the Guises and the policy of the Queen-mother.

The whispers of the crowd were checked again, by a sign from the Duc de Guise, and in the silence that followed the first name was called out,[1] and the first head fell—and still the Psalm that had begun again was chanted by the knot of prisoners, and grew fainter as their number lessened and the axe kept falling fast. The young King grew pale at the sight of so much blood, the very headsman wearied of his task, for the axe's edge was dull and blunted. Condé could keep still no longer. "Ah, what an easy task," he cried, "for foreigners to seize on France after the death of so many honourable men !" The Guises never forgot the words, and hated the Prince until his death.

The very crowd beneath them was murmuring at the sight of such unflinching courage, and as the last victim mounted to the block with the lines of the old Psalm upon his lips, there was a universal movement which even the agitated King could not misunderstand —but it was too late ; the Cardinal had made the fatal sign and the last head fell with the rest.[2]

[1] Jean Louis Albéric, Baron de Raunay.
[2] Michel Jean Louis, Baron de Castelnau Chalosse. The brother of

The Guises were fairly maddened with blood ; gallows and scaffold were not enough for them ; heads were stuck upon the railings of the castle, the markets were befouled with the dead bodies, the Loire rolled thick with human corpses, the château and the woods were crammed with dead : a man was brought in while De Guise was breakfasting, hung by the neck to the window-bars, and sent with a stab to join the others.

The whole place reeked like a shambles, so that the Queen-mother, persuaded by the softer spirits of her Court, left Amboise at last, and riding through the woods still filled with ghastly traces of the massacre, carried off the young King and Queen to forget the heretics in fresh riots and debauchery at Chenonceaux.[1]

Only one among the Guises had shown any compassion for the martyrs, Anne d'Este, the daughter of Renée de France and the Duke of Ferrara, and mother of Madame de Montpensier and Henri

this man had already laid down his life for the royal family at Amboise. One night when Francis I. and all his Court were in bed, the Duke of Orleans roused his companions and made a wanton assault on the band of lacqueys who were on guard at the bridge ; the duke would have been killed in the scuffle had not M. de Castelnau rushed in, received the blow, and died.

[1] " À huit ans et demi le père mena son fils (Agrippa d'Aubigné) à Paris, et en passant par Amboise un jour de foire, il veit les testes de ses compagnons d'Amboise encore recognoissables sur un bout de potence, et fut tellement esmu, qu'entre sept ou huit milles personnes, il s'écria — *Ils ont descapité la France les bourreaux.*" — *Œuvres Complètes de d'Aubigné*, ed. Réaume et de Causade, p. 67.

le Balafré. She was at first instinctively hostile to the Florentine who had been so unexpectedly raised to the throne of France, but she ended in being weakened by her influence, and by the strength of the family into which she had married. But the Duke Francis could not completely change the gentle nature of his wife which she inherited from the princess her mother. "This is a piteous tragedy," she cried to Catherine de Medicis, who noticed her faltering at the sight of the executions; "some great misfortune will surely fall upon our house in vengeance for it." Her husband rated her soundly for her weakness. The horrible scenes of the massacre of Vassy were yet to come, and pass before her very eyes without a possibility of hindrance, Catherine de Medicis and the Guises were to have yet another wholesale slaughter, for Amboise and Vassy were not enough, and the night of St. Bartholomew was needed to satisfy them; but the assassin Poltrot justified her fears, and after her husband had been murdered, her son Henry paid the penalty for the sins of his house in the chamber of the King at Blois.

And at this time the position of this extraordinary family might well have pardoned them their pride. The Duke Francis had gained an easy military reputation at Metz and Calais, his father before him had served his country in the field and made every use of the position which his successes gave him, his mother was Antoinette de Bourbon,

the great-aunt of Henry IV., his niece, Marie Stuart,
was on the throne of France. The Cardinal, his
brother, absorbed the rest of the power which Francis
left untouched ; he was called " the Pope across the
Alps," and treated his " colleague " at Rome on a
basis of equality. He was as eloquent in speech as
he was learned in theology, and finally had absolutely under his control three great religious orders
who throughout France and Italy worked his will
without question.[1]

Little wonder that when once so terribly em-
barked upon a definite policy the Guises felt themselves strong enough to pursue it to the bitter end.
The rank and file had been taught a sharp lesson ; it
remained to deal with the leaders. In their rage
against the Prince of Condé, who never gave any
justification for their attacks, they had even suggested
to the little King that he should stab the Prince
with his dagger while pretending to be jesting with
him, and they put down his scruples to the cowardice
of a half-grown child. At last they got him to summon Condé formally into the royal presence, while
their officials searched his baggage for incriminating
evidence—too much ashamed of their mean task to
look closely, and finding absolutely nothing. The
intrepid hunchbacked Prince appeared at once, and

---

[1] The reputation of this family is shown by the famous story of the
beggar who, as one of them passed by and gave him gold, cried, " Ah !
that must be Jesus Christ or the Cardinal de Lorraine ! "

demanding a full court to hear what he had to say, boldly gave his accusers the lie, saving the honour of the Royal Family, and declared himself ready to uphold his word by single combat. This straightforward method checked the Guises for a time ; the Duke was even compelled to pose as his champion, and must have looked almost as ridiculous as did his accomplice, Catherine, in the disguise of a sympathiser with the reformed religion.

Condé was allowed to go unharmed for the time, and Coligny was sent to Normandy. The Constable had managed to skilfully veil any real expression of opinion in Paris, by an ambiguous speech that committed him with neither party.

The first terror of surprise into which the Guises had been thrown when the plot was revealed to them had shown them one thing clearly, that it was impossible to put off holding the States-General. They determined to make this distasteful necessity fit in with the rest of their schemes, and having secured the King and the Court at Orleans, and filled the town with armed men, they proceeded to entice Navarre, and Condé by every means their unscrupulousness suggested, to attend the meeting of the Parliament. The princes of the blood came, in spite of every warning ; and trusting themselves unhesitatingly to the protection of the King, were immediately arrested, and would have certainly been executed but for the sudden death of Francis II.

This unlooked - for *contretemps* ruined for the
time being the Guises' combinations, and they were
obliged to have recourse to a fresh line of policy.
The famous League was formed, and the foundations
laid for that long civil war which was meant to end
in the supremacy of the house of Lorraine. By
skilfully posing as the party of the nation, of the
Bourgeoisie, and the Catholic religion, and by describing their opponents as aristocrats who favoured the
doctrines of the heretics, they for a time maintained
the upper hand ; for, though they themselves were
backed by foreign help, the opposition could, no more
than the Guises, describe itself as the national party.
Nor was that opposition fortunate in its leaders.
Coligny alone was worthy of the cause for which he
died ; Navarre was fickle, useless, and untrustworthy ;
Condé, with all his courage, was but little better.   It
was not until Jeanne d'Albret brought her son into
the camp after the battle of Jarnac that a real leader
appeared, and the party of the Politiques became
the party of the nation.   It was not until the Leaguers
were seen to be the really hostile and foreign element
in the struggle that in Henry of Navarre was recognised the true head of the party of France and of
the throne, and the distracted kingdom at last had
rest under a rule that was strong enough to crush all
opposition.

The history of Amboise stops with this last
tragedy, whose progress and results we have just

sketched. One more conspiracy it was yet to see—the results of the murder of Le Balafré at Blois—but its details are of no more importance than the scoundrels who engaged in it.

Almost the last personage of interest whom Amboise was to receive within its walls, was Fouquet the Surintendant, who was carried here by D'Artagnan after the marvellous chase and capture which all readers of Dumas remember.

Long years after, the room from which the executions had been witnessed served as a prison for Abd-el-Kader, many of whose suite lie buried in the gardens. Small wonder that in such a dwelling even the lovely views across the valley of the Loire could not console them for the warmer breezes of their native land.

The Franco-German war is responsible for the loss of the great " Bois de Cerf," which for so many centuries had been the wonder of the Castle. In 1577 Girolamo Lippomano saw three men lift them with difficulty from their place; and in 1644 John Evelyn writes : " In the ancient chapell (at Ambois) is a stag's head or branches, hung up by chayns, consisting of twenty brow antlers, the beame bigger than a man's middle, and of an incredible length. Indeed it is monstrous, and I cannot conceive how it should be artificial ; they show also the ribs and vertebræ of the same beast ; but these might be made of whalebone."

It remained for a German soldier to discover that they were a gigantic fraud in wood. Before the " rude conquerors " could get their booty to the next station, the famous horns had crumbled into a mass of worm-eaten dust.

And now this mediæval hoax has vanished, there is scarcely anything to be seen in the interior of Amboise. The energies of modern proprietors have been chiefly directed to removing the monstrosities of former occupants in the last two centuries ; but the work of restoration has stopped incomplete, and we could only notice with satisfaction the efforts begun to clear away the woodwork which had been built up to separate the old spacious apartments into more numerous and meaner rooms. But the outside of the castle brings an ample recompense. From no place we had yet seen were the views so numerous and so magnificent ; for even the high keep of Loches lost all that Amboise gained in the wide sweep of the Loire that flowed past its battlements to the Bridge of Tours, whose cathedral the more keen-sighted of us could discover to the west.

Before leaving the town we strolled through the shady wall along the quay to St. Denis, a cross church with a massive central tower, in Romanesque and transitional style, with very fine detail in the carving of the pillars ; and as we crossed the bridge again, the Queen of Navarre's story came into our memory of the poor muleteer who, coming home from Blois, found his wife murdered at her door, across the river. It seemed impossible to leave Amboise without some terrible impression of sudden death ; for we were passing the very spot where La Renaudie's body had been lifted in the wind — a warning to all conspirators who fail.

CHAPTER XVII

LA REINE MARGOT

"Voir la cour sans voir Marguerite de Valois, c'est ne voir ni la France ni la cour."

"Behold his bed . . . threescore valiant men are about it, they all hold swords, being expert in war : every man hath his sword girt upon his thigh because of fear in the night."

FROM Amboise the story of Touraine moves on to Blois, from Francis II. trembling above the scaffold of the Huguenots to Henry III. spurning with his foot the face of murdered Guise. Many and strange had been the changes of fortune before Le Balafré's ambition met so terrible an end. The Condé whom we saw at Amboise had fallen at Jarnac nine years afterwards ; the unstable Antoine of Navarre was dead ; Jeanne d'Albret, the noblest woman of her time, had brought her young son Henry, Prince of Béarn, to be the head of the Huguenot party, though he was as yet too young for much more settled policy than affection for his mother and young Condé, and obedience to the brave Coligny.

But into the heartbreaking struggle of the civil

wars we cannot enter. It is but possible for us to look swiftly at the troublous reign of Charles IX. through the medium of the writings of another Marguerite, another and the last child of Catherine de Medicis, " not less divine but more human in her moods" than the gentle, mystic sister of King Francis.

From her we shall learn the life of that Court which still wandered so often to the pleasant castles of Touraine, from the reeking atmosphere of Paris and the Louvre. It is joined with her name that there first comes into prominence the young King of Navarre, who shall at last bring order into the chaos of conflicting parties ; it is in company with her that we shall hear, from very close at hand, the clamour of that tocsin of St. Bartholomew, whose echoes troubled every town in France ; and we shall be listening to the most celebrated woman of her time, to a princess gifted with the beauty of an Aphrodite, the refinement of a Valois, and a loyalty that was all her own.

The life of Marguerite began in the Court of Catherine of Medicis, in the company of the " esca- dron volant " and such ladies as Madame de Nevers and Charlotte de Beaune Semblançay, granddaughter of the unhappy Semblançay, executed in the reign of Francis I., a slight, fair - haired woman, by turns sparkling with vivacity and languishing with a gentle weakness, wife of Simon de Fizes, Baron de Sauves, and afterwards of François de la Trémouille, Marquis de Noirmoutier.

In 1569 came news from Henry, Duc d'Anjou, that threw the whole Court into a bustle of preparation. A battle was imminent, and he must see his mother and the King before he fought. The journey from Paris to Tours was done in three and a half days, and the ladies seem to have derived much amusement from the distress caused to poor Cardinal de Bourbon,[1] whose constitution was little fitted for such unwonted exertions.

It was in the park of Plessis-lez-Tours, at this time, that the childhood of Marguerite first consciously ended, and her brother secured her help and friendship by treating her as a woman grown up and responsible, who should help his interests with the King and with their mother. "Such language," she writes, "was quite new to me. My life hitherto had been quite thoughtless; my only cares the dance and hunting. I had even neglected my dress and personal appearance."[2] Her life was henceforth to be among the society described by Brantôme, "whose vices it would be repulsive to suggest, whose virtues were homicide and adultery,"[3] where "no man was honoured who could not show blood on his hands,

---

[1] Charles de Bourbon, Archbishop of Rouen, son of the Duke of Vendôme, called King Charles X. by the League. He would be about forty-six at this time, and died twenty-one years later.

[2] *Mémoires de la Reine Marguerite*, Bibl. Elzevir., P. Jannet, 1858.

[3] Swinburne, *Miscellanies* ("Mary Queen of Scots"), p. 376.

no woman admired who would not boast as loudly
of the favours she had granted, as her gallants of the
favours they had received."

In such a court, where ignorance was impossible,
innocence was almost as rare ; and this latest addition
to the beauties of the "escadron volant" soon received
the approval of her companions in some very credit-
able scandals which were in circulation about her
various intrigues almost immediately after her appearance in public. The Aurora or the Cytherea of the
lesser poets of the Court, the Pasithée of Ronsard's
verses, she had rapidly taken her place as the acknowledged queen of the many revels of that disastrous
time ; and indeed at the age of eighteen she seems to
have easily surpassed even the loveliest sirens in that
band whom Catherine de Medicis had gathered round
her, of the fairest faces in the land, for the bewilder-
ment of the gallant captains and politicians of
France.

Her thick black hair shaded a face of brilliant
whiteness, and from beneath long dark lashes her
eyes shone suddenly as the delicate red lips moved
in speech, and with words of no common kind too,
but witty with the unrestrained freedom of her time,
and with a learning whose facility and skill were a
perpetual amazement to her companions.

Small wonder that her name soon was whispered
in connection with that of the leader of the Catholic
party, Henri de Guise, the head of the faction with

whom she was thrown most in contact. At twenty-two years of age the young Duke of Guise had well-nigh reached the level of his father Francis's fame ; the height and elegance of his figure, the natural majesty of his looks and bearing, seemed to confirm the popular opinion which already idolised the son of the great captain, and which was to support him afterwards in his ambitious and ill-fated struggle for the throne of France.

Unfortunately for Marguerite, her own *Mémoires* are not the only sources open to us for information as to her character and her methods ; but it seems fairly clear that this, probably her first, love was at any rate sincere. She can as little hide her admiration for De Guise at this time, as she can conceal her passionate feelings for the brave Bussy d'Amboise later on ; and she deserves at least such compassion from her judges as shall be always given to a nature keenly susceptible, little liking restraint, and sacrificed mercilessly upon the altar of political necessity.

Her vexation at the insinuations of Du Guast[1] at this time brought on a fever, in which she was tended by her favourite brother the King ; for the royal physicians had themselves been stricken with the disorder. To rid herself of similar persecution in the future, she besought her sister Claude, now

---

[1] He was assassinated in 1575. No writer of the sixteenth century would have deprived Marguerite's reputation of the honour of his death, so it is put down to her.

Duchess of Lorraine, to arrange the marriage of
Henri de Guise with Catherine de Clèves, Princesse
de Porcian, which was celebrated in 1571. The
House of Lorraine was already but too closely connected with the royal family ; any further alliance
was impossible.

But other reasons, still more important, had
already settled the destinies of Marguerite. Peace
had been made with the Huguenots after Jarnac
and Montcontour ; and an attempt at securing the
head of the rebel party by a close alliance with the
throne was only what might have been expected
from the characteristic political methods of Catherine.
It was even rumoured that unless prompt measures
were taken, the young Béarnais would soon be betrothed to the English Elizabeth,[1] for whom Catherine
had already arranged, in her own mind, a match with
the Duc d'Anjou. The King was as determined as
the rest, and spoke with some levity of the tardiness
with which the Pope gave his approval. Margot
should be married at any cost, and his own royal
hand should give her away.

The opposite party in politics were equally delighted, and Jeanne d'Albret, after her first and very
natural disgust at the habits of the Court, managed
the negotiations with a skill and intrepidity which
deserved a better fate ; for after returning to Paris
from her visit to the Court in Touraine, she sickened

[1] See M. H. de la Ferrière, *Le XVIme Siècle et les Valois.*

suddenly and died—of a pleurisy, so it was given out ; but rumours were persistently spread that her death was owing to the scent of some gloves skilfully prepared by Réné, the Queen's Florentine perfumer ; and these reports gained credence from the fact that Ambroise Paré, in his examination of the body, was forbidden to look at the brain, the sole organ that Réné's poisons would have touched. Be this as it may, Jeanne d'Albret was too good a woman for her existence to be long tolerated ; her honesty, like Semblançay's long before, was too transparent, her truth too courageous, for life among the Court of Catherine de Medicis, and when her duty to her son brought her into contact with that Court, she was only allowed to live long enough to complete the negotiations, and not too long for the interests of the Queen-mother. She is one of the few women of her time whose death it is possible, for every reason, to regret.[1]

In August 1572 the marriage of Henry of Navarre to Marguerite de Valois was celebrated with great splendour at the Louvre ; and surely there was never a festival at which political necessity so

---

[1] It will be remembered that Jeanne was the daughter of our first Marguerite d'Angoulême, Queen of Navarre, the author of the *Hepta-meron*. It was for Isabeau, her fascinating aunt, that Clement Marot, a favourite with her mother, wrote some of his most charming lines.

"Elle a très bien cette gorge d'albastre,
Ce doux parler, ce cler teint, ces beaux yeux,
Mais en effet ce petit ris folastre
C'est, à mon gré, ce qui lui sied le mieux."

triumphed over human feelings, not only in the principal pair concerned, but in nearly all the spectators. For the young King of Navarre had to stifle his genuine grief for his mother's sudden death, his wife had to conceal her own passions beneath the mask of a proper conjugal affection, no less had Condé to forgive D'Anjou his father's murder, and the young Duc de Guise to forget Poltrot de Méré. Opinions were strangely divided, for even the Catholics themselves realised that something more was in progress than they could fathom, and the Huguenots still felt uneasy, they knew not why. So little could the Princess conquer her repugnance at the last moment to the marriage forced upon her, that the King was obliged with his own hand to bend her head down in token of assent during the ceremony. Neither husband nor wife treated that ceremony as anything save the mockery it really was; and they went their own way, bound yet divided, to the end.

The sole link that ever bound them was the same political necessity which had first brought about their marriage ; and to this political necessity (though to this only) Marguerite remained for ever loyal. Her husband was no very brilliant example of conjugal fidelity ; and the accepted lover of Madame de Sauves could not severely criticise the mistress of De Guise.

Thus their strange married life began. The first

interruption to the fêtes and dances was the "accident" to Coligny, when he was wounded in the shoulder by Maurevel's pistol-shot from a window in the Louvre. It was connected by public opinion with the old ill-founded quarrel between Guise and Coligny about the murder of Duke Francis;[1] and for a while all seemed quiet again.

What followed is a matter of history too well known, too wide in scope, for these chapters to relate. We can but look upon one small part of the great tragedy of St. Bartholomew, the part that came beneath the actual notice of Marguerite, so lately married, and from that infer the horrors of the rest.

The resolution to massacre the Huguenots was taken on the 23d of August 1572. Catherine's sole object seems to have been to allow both parties to cut each other's throats and leave the throne the stronger for their fall. Marguerite tells us what really turned the brain of the poor passionate King : "The Huguenots were coming to accuse Guise" of attempting Coligny's murder. De Retz had to explain who were the real culprits, with hints perhaps of another Sicilian Vespers, and other such inventions as the Italians with Catherine de Medicis would employ to fire Charles's unsteady imagination. He suddenly and wildly gave

---

[1] The original still exists (Bib. Nat. MS. F. 209, fo. 37) of the act by which the children of Duke Francis accept the King's decree as to the innocence of Coligny of their father's murder by Poltrot.

his consent, and at four the next morning Besme, the brutal follower of the Guises, had thrown Coligny's corpse from the upper window to the feet of his master, who stood waiting in the court.

Of all this Marguerite was told nothing. Her first suspicion of the truth came as she went to bed on the night of the council. Her sister Claude clung to her with tears, beseeching her not to go; but Catherine sternly bade her twice be off to her own room. Arrived there, and praying to be saved from the unknown dangers which she felt around her, she found the husband she had married but a week ago waiting upon his bed, who ordered her to lie down. "This I did," she writes, "and then found that his bed was surrounded by some thirty or forty Huguenots whom I did not know ; for it was but a few days since my marriage. All night they talked of nothing but the mishap which had befallen the admiral, resolving as soon as day should break to demand justice on Guise from the King, in default of which they would do justice themselves.

" As for me, the tears of my sister continued to trouble my heart, and I could not sleep for the fear which she had given me, though of what I knew not. So the night passed, and I never closed my eyes. At daybreak the King, my husband, said that he was minded to go and play tennis with King Charles, and then and there to ask his justice. He left my room, and all the gentlemen with him. I saw that

it was day, and thinking that the peril of which my
sister spoke was past, being heavy with sleep, I told
my nurse to shut the door that I might sleep at
my ease." Meanwhile the tocsin which gave the
signal for the massacre had rung from St. Germain
l'Auxerrois, Coligny was past all human justice, and
the Louvre itself soon became little better than a
shambles.

"An hour afterwards," goes on the Princess,
"when I had fallen into a deep sleep, there came
suddenly a man beating with his hands and feet
against my door, crying, 'Navarre, Navarre!' My
nurse, thinking it was the King, my husband, ran
swiftly and opened the door. It was a gentleman
called M. de Léran,[1] who had a sword-thrust in the
shoulder, and a wound from a pike in the arm ; he
was pursued by four archers, and they all rushed after
him into my room. He threw himself upon my bed
for safety. Feeling his hold upon me I threw myself into the space between the bed and the wall ;
he followed, keeping fast hold of my body. I knew
nothing of the man, and could not discover whether
he was there to harm me, or whether the archers
were in pursuit of him or of myself; so both of us
cried out, the one as frightened as the other. At
last, by God's will, M. de Nançay, Captain of the

---

[1] Readers of Dumas know better : it was La Mole flying from
Coconnas and the rest, and taking refuge with the woman who was
afterwards to give him her love, as she gave him pity now. Compare
the scene in *La Reine Margot.*

Guard, came in, and finding me in such a plight
could not, for all his pity, stay his laughter; with
sharp reprimands to the archers for their indiscretion
he ordered them forth, and granted me the life of the
poor man who still was clasping me—him I made
to lie down, and gave him remedies in my own
cabinet until such time as he was quite cured.
While I changed my clothes, for I was all covered
with blood, M. de Nançay told me what was going
on, and assured me that my husband was in the
King's chamber and would suffer no harm. Making
me put on a dressing-gown, he led me to the room
of my sister, the Duchesse de Lorraine, where I came
more dead than alive; for as I crossed the ante-
chamber, whose doors were wide open, a gentleman
named Bourse, flying from the archers who pursued
him, was run through within a few paces from me. I
fell half-unconscious into the arms of M. de Nançay
on the other side, thinking for the moment that the
same blow had wounded both of us." . .

In her sister's bedroom she begged for the lives
of two gentlemen in her husband's suite, which were
with difficulty granted her; others were less successful, for the King's brain had given way at the sight
of blood, and he was little better than a madman.
The scenes outside the Louvre were worse still.
Tavannes was slaying like a butcher; Montpensier
like a fanatic; De la Rochefoucauld, who thought the
whole thing one more of the wild King's jests, had

his throat cut in the middle of a scream of laughter ;
few like young Caumont de la Force were so fortunate as to escape, sheltered beneath the dead
bodies of his brother and his father.

The harvest of death went on, throughout Paris,
throughout France, until the whole nation seemed
smitten as by a pestilence. Coligny, the one pure-
minded politician-soldier, was murdered ; Goujon, the
artist, was killed even at his work ; Ramus, the philo-
sopher, was dead ; L'Hôpital had died of grief ; and
the morality, the religion of the nation was dead
with them. A week after the massacre a great flock
of crows and ravens settled upon the Louvre, and
for days afterwards the King seemed to hear the
shrieks of dying men around the palace.

Some annoyance was felt that, amid all this blood-
shedding, both Navarre and Condé had come forth
scot-free, and the plots began again ; but Marguerite
would not desert her husband, or consent to a divorce.
La Mole and Coconnas, puppets in the hands
of stronger wills, paid for their loyalty with their
lives, and the sadness of Marguerite grew deeper still
at the loss of her favourite brother, the King, " tout
l'appuy et support de ma vie, un frère duquel je
n'avois receu que bien." The next reign belongs
to other chapters, but there are one or two more
pages of the *Mémoires* of Marguerite, one or two
more incidents in her life, which cannot be passed
over.

It is in 1574 that "the brave Bussy d'Amboise" is first mentioned. "He was born," she says, "to be the terror of his enemies, the glory of his master, and the hope of his friends ; " and there is little doubt that he helped to console Marguerite for her husband's absence ; it was only five years afterwards that his love for the Countess of Montsoreau was so terribly punished by her husband. But political reasons again proved superior to sentiment in the life of this somewhat hardly-used princess.

Life at the Court became unbearable when war had been openly declared against her husband outside, so she left Paris to help the affairs of her brother D'Alençon in Flanders.

" I travelled," she tells us, " in a litter made with pillars covered with pink Spanish velvet, broidered with gold, and adorned with devices worked in silk ; the litter was fitted with glass too, and covered with devices,"—some forty of them, all speaking of the sun and of its effects.

They went to Liège by way of the Meuse in charming boats, but the pleasure of the whole party was suddenly stopped by unforeseen disasters—first by the rising of the river, which obliged them all to fly for safety up the mountain-side, and then by the sudden illness of a maid-of-honour, Mademoiselle de Tournon. For the romantic story of this young lady's love and death, the tender-hearted reader is referred to Marguerite's own words ; they would lose too much

in the rendering to permit of their transcription
here.[1]

The account of her journey continues to be full
of interest. Huy, some six miles from Liège, proves
a most inhospitable resting-place, for they drew
chains across the streets, and pointed cannon at the
Princess's lodging all the night. At Dinan, farther
on, the burgomasters had just been elected, "tout
y estoit ce jour là en debauche, tout le monde
yvre;" and Marguerite's cortège was kept outside
the gates while the drunken citizens threw away their
cups and seized what arms were near to oppose her
entry. At last she rose in her litter, took off her
mask, and beckoned to the most important of them
that she wished to speak with him. After some
trouble it was arranged that part of her escort should
be allowed with her inside the town.

Unluckily, a servant of the bishop's was recognised among them—and the Bishop of Liège was
an especial foe—so in a moment all was tumult
and disorder again. A drunken deputation came up
to Madame la Princesse, apparently with the object

---

[1] Notice particularly the scene where her ungrateful lover meets her
corpse being borne out for burial ; he is told that it is Mademoiselle de
Tournon—"à ce mot, il se pasme et tombe. Il le fault emporter en un
logis comme mort, voulant plus justement, en cette extrémité, luy rendre
union en la mort, que trop tard en la vie il luy avoit accordée. Son
âme, que je crois, allant dans le tombeau requerir pardon à celle que
son desdaigneux oubly y avoit mise, le laissa quelque temps sans
aucune apparence de vie ; d'où estant revenu, l'anima de nouveau
pour luy faire esprouver la mort, qui d'une seule fois n'eust assez puni
son ingratitude."

of protesting against the bishop, but scarcely able
to utter anything intelligible at all. The oldest
of them, stuttering and smiling, asked her whether
she was a friend of the Comte de Lalain, and her
answer that she was not only friend but relation too,
restored everything to a complacent state of baccha-
nalian friendship. During the night the poor Princess's enemies were active. Du Bois, the King's
agent, had arrived, and was hard at work plotting to
get Marguerite into the power of the Spaniards, and
the town into the hands of Don Juan.

But her good friends the burgomasters, having
slept off their wine, had not forgotten their promises
of friendship, and helped her willingly to escape.
So when Du Bois arrived to lead her to Namur, with
feigned complaisance she left the town in his company, with several hundreds of the citizens escorting
her as well ; and by dint of carefully watching and
talking to him, she managed to progress in exactly the
opposite direction, to embark herself and her litters
on the river, and finally to put the stream between
her followers and the Spaniards, much to Du Bois's
disgust, who only realised too late the cool audacity
of the whole proceeding, and was left storming with
anger on the wrong bank amid an amused crowd of
citizens from Dinan. With many more adventures
she at last travelled by way of Cambresis and Chas-
telet to her own La Fère, where her brother was
waiting for her.

But they were soon obliged to return to Paris to the old intrigues ; they arrived in time for St. Luc's marriage with Jeanne de Brissac, at which D'Anjou was so insulted by the "mignons" of the King. The Prince's situation at the Court had become intolerable again, and Marguerite began to plot for his escape. With some difficulty she managed to let him down from a window in the Louvre with a rope ladder ; it became necessary to conceal all traces of the flight, so her maids put the ladder on the fire ; it made so great a blaze that the chimney itself caught, and in a few moments the royal archers were clamouring at the door to be let in, and extinguish the blaze. They were with difficulty prevailed on " to leave the princess asleep," and let her maids put out the fire, and so the danger passed. At last Marguerite herself left the Court for Gascony " et ce petit Genève de Pau," where she found her husband ill, and nursed him tenderly. Several months at Nérac followed " où nostre cour estoit si belle et si plaisante, que n'envi-ons point celle de France." If reports were right, Chancellor Pibrac helped the Princess to pass the time here ; and Chicot has left upon record how the young Turenne (then Duc de Bouillon) was also gracefully allowed to fall in love with her catholic-minded majesty ; Henry himself beguiled the time with La Fosseuse, and the war that followed could have borne no more appropriate name than that of " La Guerre des Amoureux."

It ended in the treaty of Fleix. And after the failure of her favourite brother's expedition in Flanders, and his death (from the fatal bouquet of Diane de Montsoreau), Marguerite returned to Nérac from her short visit to the Court in 1583, and left her husband again after his excommunication by the Pope two years later. A short and stormy visit to Agen followed, and then she disappears within the Château d'Usson, one of the old prisons of Louis XI. in Auvergne. Here the civil wars of 1588 passed her by unharmed, though two years later the royal troops of her husband chased the Leaguers from the field before her very eyes ; and so for many more years the actual Queen of France lived in seclusion, refusing constantly to grant her husband a divorce while Gabrielle d'Estrées is living, but after her death (in 1599) consenting to the Italian marriage.

Though she came again to Paris, she still lived in close retirement until her death some sixteen years later—a retirement which, by her friends, is called a literary and cultured retreat ; by her enemies a debauch of wickedness sheltered by the seclusion of her various palaces ; and of a like mixed nature is the estimate of her character that has been handed down to us.

As her beauty is of that mould which was apparently more in favour three centuries ago than now, so her morals can with even greater difficulty

be made to conform with any modern standard
of decorum ; but as a type of the Court lady of
her time she is unapproachable. With an accurate
knowledge of the powers her beauty gave her,
and a careful economy of its resources, she tried
to live out, according to her knowledge, that life
of sentiment, of passion, of sheer human nature,
which had well-nigh been crushed out of her at
the beginning by the relentless policy of the
Queen-mother. Amidst the depravity and corruption of the most shameless Court in Europe, her
intellect and her refinement were as rare as they
were worthy of respect ; and if we had only her
own *Mémoires* to guide us, our estimate of her
character and her worth would be a very different
one—with so much grace are they written, with
so much insight and skill are the events of a
distracted time described. Such women as Jeanne
d'Albret are rare in the sixteenth century ; a
Marguerite de Valois is needed to complete the
picture—a woman who, to the virtues of the Valois
added but a small part of their vices, who of all
the children of Catherine de Medicis is the one
posterity could least have spared.

ENTRANCE AND BASSE COUR OF THE CHÂTEAU OF BLOIS, showing the façade of Louis XII., and his statue above the gateway

CHAPTER XVIII

BLOIS

"J'avance parmi les décombres
De tout un monde enseveli,
Dans le mystère des pénombres
A travers des limbes d'oubli."
                                    GAUTIER.

BALZAC was afraid that later generations would know nothing of the Château of Blois save from his pages ; so far advanced, in his day, was the ruin and decay of the whole fabric. But that ruin has been suddenly and thoroughly arrested ; the hand of the conscientious restorer has intervened, and that with a lavishness of display, an ingenuity of detail, very rarely equalled. The " buried world," upon which three centuries of kindly time had laid their touch, has been refashioned in a somewhat garish blaze of gold and carving ; there are but few " mysterious shadows " in these brightly-coloured rooms ; there is but little left to fancy, to the dreams of the imagination, in a reconstruction so painfully complete.

Yet it is difficult to find fault with that spirit of

almost reverential care which has given us back the
great Castle of Pierrefonds, with all its intricacies of
defence, which has restored the walls of wondrous
Carcassonne, which has preserved the marvels upon
Mont St. Michel ; and of the two extremes, Blois is
perhaps nearer to what is possible for us of perfection
than is Chinon, deserted, ruined past recall.   To few
houses is it given as to Langeais, or Azay-le-Rideau,
to escape decay and yet preserve the mellowed beauty
of their past—a beauty like the golden haze upon a
famous picture, or the strange bloom upon an antique
marble, which is something different from any hues
or colourings wrought by the hand of man.

But at Blois no change, no renovation can check
the rush of memories that press upon the traveller
directly he has crossed the threshold beneath the
statue of the good King Louis, for the threefold
fashion of the architecture around him speaks elo-
quently of the three great ages through which the
life of the castle has passed.   The early years when
the Orleans princes were educated here, and Valentine
Visconti mourned her murdered husband ; the terrible
days of the sixteenth century, when Guise was
murdered above the exquisite carvings of the central
staircase ; finally, the decaying glories of Gaston and
his daughter, fitly framed in the ruled lines and
spaces of the frigid building opposite the entrance.

The first view of Blois from the town shows the
outside of the wing of Francis I., ending at the right

hand corner in the great tower which was half destroyed when Mansard joined his later buildings on to the older fabric ; the whole stands on a rising slope ; and beneath the fine buttresses, upon which the wing of Gaston rests, the road plunges deeply into a dark ravine which winds downward to the Church of St. Sauveur, and was once the bed of a stream that joined the waters of the Loire.

The entrance to the château is to the left of Francis's wing, along a winding terrace that leads to a quiet moss-grown square, the old basse-cour into which Raoul rode with letters to the prince, and where the son of Charles the Poet heard the soldiers shouting that the Duke of Orleans was the King of France. There is his statue as Louis XII. above the entrance-gate,[1] with the badge of the porcupine beneath it, which he took from the " camail " that his father wore at Agincourt ; and in the inner court, to which the gateway leads, the line of lightly chiselled columns that support the painted roof immediately beyond is also the work of this King, who did much for the improvement of the old feudal fortress which the Dukes of Orleans inherited from the Counts of Blois. The oldest work of all is on the left side of the great court, by the chapel which saw the consecration of Joan of Arc's banner, and the betrothal of

[1] Not the original, which was destroyed at the Revolution. " The father of his people " was not good enough.

Margot to Henry of Navarre ; the only other
remnant of the earlier fabric is the apartment in
which the States-General were assembled in the
reign of Henry III.   Contrary to the general rule
(says M. Viollet le Duc) that all great halls in
palaces or châteaux should be composed of two
floors, this one is built wholly on the ground-floor,
and has no rooms beneath it ; it is separated into
two parts by a line of columns, and roofed by a
double row of vaulted arches ; it is not by any
means an imposing room—nor, indeed, could the
château itself, in the thirteenth century, have been at
all a striking edifice—and it is scarcely helped by the
extraordinary scheme of colour and pattern which the
modern architect has spread regardlessly over its walls.

This council hall was reached by the King
through a private staircase leading from the wing
of Francis I., the wing to the right hand of the
entrance, whose exterior we, like La Fontaine, had
seen from the great square in the town outside.   It
is this wing that contains the gem of the whole
castle—the "escalier à jour" that springs, many-sided,
from the sculptured wall and lights up all the court
with the exquisite beauty of its lines and carvings.
Of the whole architecture of this wing, by an unknown artist, as so often happens in Touraine, there
is an excellent description by Mrs. Mark Pattison.[1]
" The main features," says this writer, " are such as

[1] *Renaissance of Art in France*, vol. i. p. 51.

are common to other châteaux in the valley of the
Loire ; but there are important though minor
differences which specially individualise it. The
architectural scheme is very simple. Three rows
of pilasters are superimposed one above the other.
At about two-thirds down the front the open spiral
staircase juts out and towers upwards. It seems at
first to stand free, breaking up the even succession
of small columns and their perpendicular descent
with the bold projection of its octagonal lines.
But above, it is embraced and caught into the whole
mass by the broad crowning cornice which gathers
within its strengthening bands every various curve.
The sculptured dormers fret along its edge, search-
ing the air with their pointed tongues, and twice the
carved cases of the chimney stacks break aloft
through the roof like towers, but the cornice keeps
firm hold upon their base." It is the grave simplicity of the wall from which the staircase springs,
the fine and choice instinct of proportion which it
displays, says the same writer, that mark this building as a production of the new movement, as an
advance on Chenonceaux and Langeais.

The staircase itself is a triumph of ingenuity—

> "Carved with figures strange and sweet,
> All made out of the carver's brain,"

a perfect whole, for which a master mind drew the
first plans, and every detail was carefully and
lovingly worked out.

The figures poised above the entrance, though they have been for three hundred years out of doors, still preserve the clear, firm touch of their unknown sculptor's chisel, and there is little doubt that these statues are either some of the first work of Jean Goujon in his youth, or are the productions of that school by which he was first and most directly influenced. Everything of unknown origin at this period is generally put down to this artist, but in this case there are certain indications of style which seem to lend somewhat more of certainty to a conjecture usually a trifle reckless. The date of Goujon's best work is considerably later than the time at which the wing of Francis I. was built; yet so elaborate a piece of architecture as this staircase may very well have remained without the statues that completed it until long after all the surroundings had been finished. There are several stones in it that to this day are quite untouched, a few are only roughly chiselled out ; the end of the sixteenth century was too hurried in its methods to allow the perfect completion of a structure for which, as there seems reason to believe, the initial ideas may have been sketched quite early in the reign of Francis I.

Goujon was born in 1520,[1] and it is quite

[1] For the date of Goujon's birth see *Archives de l'Art Français*, by A. de Montaiglon, iii. 350. Blois was building in 1515 (L. E. de Laborde, *La Renaissance des Arts à la Cour de France*, p. 190) ; in 1540 Goujon was at Rouen. The next year he worked in St. Maclou and in the Cathedral ; in 1542 with Lescot ; two years afterwards at

possible that while still a simple mason under old Mâitre Quesnel, and before the work with Pierre Lescot at St. Germain l'Auxerrois had made him famous, the young artist chiselled these figures, or at least the one on the right hand of the entrance, which particularly recalls various mannerisms in the works that are recognised as his.

The folding clothes are held in by a belt below the actual waist, and the drapery is caught up on the swell of the hip in a way peculiarly his own, and reproduced on the famous Fontaine des Innocents, and in a bas-relief in the Salle des cent Suisses; the very attitude in which the wavy sheaf of water-flags is held is also characteristic of his methods; but more convincing still is the elaborate treatment of the head-dress, with its pendent ornament, and the chiselled bracelet upon the arm, both of which are found especially prominent in the "Diane Chasser-esse," another example of the long lithe limbs, and the small breasts high on the body, which Goujon was especially fond of reproducing. For a drawing of this statue see p. 174, and compare the frontis-piece of this volume.

The carving of the canopy of this statue at Blois is alone worthy of long study; though every detail varies, yet each contributes gracefully to the per-fection of the whole; here especially is it possible

Ecouen. The "Fons Nymphium" and the "Caryatides" were carved in 1550, and five years later he had begun the work on the Louvre at which he was employed while the massacre of St. Bartholomew was going on.

to realise what a labour of love was the work of the
old masons, what time unlimited their workmen had,
to chisel cunningly at the firm white stone beneath
the mellow sunshine of Touraine, until each part
was filled with something of the individuality of the
man whose life was spent in slow and perfect labour
with his hands, until the scheme which gave each
workman his allotted task was finished in its harmony
of carving, its strength and delicacy of construction
and of form.   It is often by the shape and mould-
ing of his mere grotesques that a great artist's power
is seen ;   and this is the case here.   Between the
statues we have just examined and the main wall is
a salamander, marvellous in its originality, its living
force of movement, clinging to the stone with a
reality that is little short of creative ; the line of its
spinal column curves firmly from neck to tail as in
a living thing, the grip of hind and fore feet set with
claws is amazing in its grasp and actuality of movement and organic strength, the very warts upon its
scaly back add one more touch of life to this extraordinary carving.

But the wonders of this perfect structure do not
cease with the sculpture upon its outward walls.   The
stairs wind upwards, folding round their central shaft
as the petals of a tulip fold one within the other,
and by a slight curve at the attachment of each
step, a strange look of life and growth is produced
that is marvellously helped by the ascending spiral

INTERIOR OF THE OPEN STAIRCASE IN THE WING OF FRANCIS I. AT BLOIS.

of the column which supports the whole ; its waving
lines rush upwards like a flame blown from beneath,
or like the flying spiral of a jet of water falling fast
yet strongly from a height ; there is in it a beauty
that is elemental, a touch of the same nature that

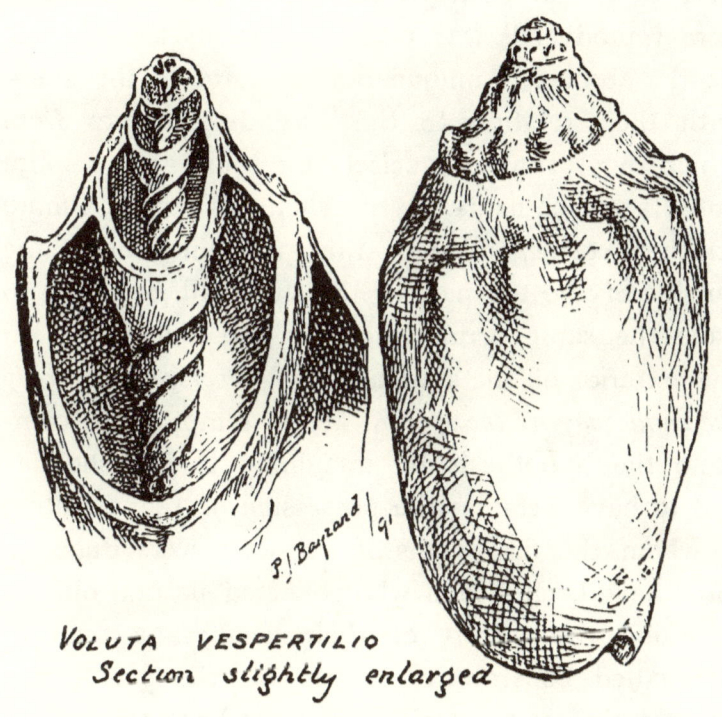

VOLUTA VESPERTILIO
Section slightly enlarged

curves the tall shaft of the iris upwards from the
pool in which it grows. But the delicate strength
of this central column reproduces with an even
greater accuracy the lines that in natural objects are
most beautiful because most adapted to the purpose
they fulfil ; the spiral upon its shaft is the exact

curve which is contained within a sea-shell,[1] for the beauty of the work is of that necessary order which comes of perfect skill, and finds its ultimate justification in the essential harmony of natural structures. In this particular case it seems more than probable that an actual shell (of the same kind as the one here reproduced) was used consciously as a model ; for the absolutely unique double curve of the steps, with their relation to the ascending curves from which they grow, is precisely the same as the spiral and · its attachments in the shell. There is a more striking correspondence still : the lines upon the outside of the top part of the shell will be found to have the same arrangement as the balustrades on the exterior of the staircase, *and reversed, in exactly the same way as the spiral.* It is tempting to complete the hypothesis by imagining such a shell as this to have been in the possession of the architect to whom the first plans of the work were due : he must have been a man who collected natural objects to study the secrets of their beauty ; a man of unequalled constructive power, for the groin-work and vaulting of the stairs is not the least astounding part of the whole building ; a man, too, of extraordinary imagination, and with a sense of harmonious proportion rarely equalled in the world. Scarcely

---

[1] It is by the kindness of Mr. C. Stewart, the President of the Linnæan Society, that I am enabled to point out this valuable detail in the workmanship of the staircase, which so far as I know is without a parallel in architecture. The exterior is reproduced on p. 165.

any one of that time save Leonardo da Vinci possessed a genius at once so universal and so thorough, and Leonardo was at Amboise, a little farther down the river, just when the first plans of this staircase would be required. Is it possible that Francis found one last sketch, one remnant of the dying artist's genius, and employed to decorate his newest château the last "tour de force" of the great master for whom he had no care to build a tomb?

It is possible to realise, even more keenly than elsewhere, the full spirit and movement of the true Renaissance, when such a gem of art and architecture as the wing of Francis I. is placed next to the cold and meaningless productions of François Mansard at the height of his reputation, at the most chilling point of his respectability. In this wing, opposite the entrance, so different from all the rest of the château, lived Gaston d'Orléans, dullest of royal dullards, himself so chillingly respectable that he had formed the plan of delivering up the whole of the palace to the mercies of reforming Mansard, and would have done so, had not Providence removed him in time and preserved for the wonder of later ages the fantasies of a creation too unfettered for his slow wit to understand.

The early history of the castle is connected with those Counts of Blois whom we have already heard of in tracing the fortunes of their mortal enemies, the Angevin Counts. Upon the remains of the old

Roman camp which held the tongue of land between the Loire and the now lost Arou, the robber captains of the sixth and seventh centuries built their first rude stronghold, which was later on to become part of the wide possessions held by the Counts of Vermandois, Champagne, and Blois. These three houses were among the first of the great feudal families of France in the eleventh and twelfth centuries; their relationships extended to lands as far apart as England and Palestine, while nearer home Flanders, Burgundy, Aquitaine, and Navarre were all more or less closely connected with the same powerful stock. It was from Thibault le Tricheur, whose fame still fills the low country all round Chambord, that the Château of Blois received its first donjon built with money raised by certain fraudulent practices, and increased by more open deeds of violence and robbery. Even if authenticated records of these times were forthcoming they would be of little interest, for the quarrels of the barons had not much influence on the real history of France; but before the thirteenth century the possessions of Champagne and Vermandois had fallen by marriage to King Philip IV., and by 1233 Chartres and Blois had been bought by the Crown from another Count Thibault. Blois had become Crown property, and was soon to be the recognised possession of the family of Orleans.

The historian Froissart, who was chaplain here

during the regency of the dukes in the first years of Charles VI.'s reign, relates an interview that took place between the Dukes of Burgundy and Berry concerning the old quarrels between Brittany and France; but the castle began to take its actual place in the history of France when Louis d'Orléans brought Valentine Visconti here from Milan.[1] The princess had made a triumphant entry into Paris, and had immediately secured the good graces of the King; but her happiness was very short-lived, and this visit to Blois, one of the many homes of her clever and unfeeling husband, seemed almost a flight from the horror of the poor King's madness, which she had tried in vain to soothe, and from the dark suspicions of the changeable populace of Paris.

About this time Eustache Deschamps, the poet, was " maître d'hôtel " to the duke, and at his marriage in 1393 received from his patron a present of five hundred gold pieces. It was by Eustache's care that the library, which had been begun by a small donation from the royal collection, was increased by the *Three Pilgrimages of Human Life, of Christ, and of the Soul*, bought from one Jehan Bizet, and written in cursive characters. There was a *Legende Dorée* too, bound in the black velvet which the duke especially affected, and a *History of the Old and New Testament* by Pierre Comestor, which had been translated in the last century, and cost the

---

[1] See Chapter VI. " Three Dukes of Orleans."

duke as much as eighty gold crowns. A book to
the taste of Madame Valentine was perhaps *La
Consolacion de Boëce*, which her husband bought
in Paris — she needed comfort as much as most
women of her time ; while the scholarly proclivi-
ties of the duke himself are traceable in the *Pro-
blesmes d'Aristote*, translated by Evrard de Conty,
which he bought from a Paris student, whose tastes
were probably more in the direction of the outspoken
rhymes with which François Villon was soon to delight the idle scholars of the capital.

But Valentine was not allowed to rest for long in
the quiet valley of the Loire. She had to rejoin the
duke, whose excess and immorality soon brought
their inevitable punishment, and in 1407 she was
once more at Blois in even greater grief than at her
former visit, for this handsome, cruel husband, whom
she had loved passionately in spite of all his faults,
had been basely murdered in the streets of Paris.
Her attempts at vengeance failed.   The poor
King's mind, which in its weakness showed more
plainly all those feelings which its strength had
hidden, was warped for ever against his brother
of Orleans ; the murder was pardoned, praised even,
and the gentle heart of Valentine was broken in
a year.

Her son Charles in his first years showed but
little of the poetic temperament which always passed
almost unnoticed by his companions.   In company

with Dunois, the famous Bastard, the most capable
of all the children of Duke Louis, he was soon at
work organising the forces which were to fall at
Agincourt. In 1415 the battle had been won and
lost, Charles had been taken prisoner, and the
Château of Blois was deserted. Twelve years afterwards even the library which had lightened the hours
of those who were left behind in mourning for their
lord was removed to Saumur for greater safety ;
for tidings had reached the duke in his captivity
of the movements of the English in the valley of
the Loire.

The castle itself was soon filled with tokens of
coming change. In 1429 Joan of Arc was in the
Church of St. Sauveur, where the Archbishop of
Rheims blessed the standard she was to bear to
victory ; and the tide of English invasion turned at
last. But the delivery of Charles d'Orléans was not
yet. Dunois was in charge of the castle when the
conspiracy of the Praguerie broke out that was
organised by the Dauphin Louis against his father
Charles VII. ; and only in 1440, after twenty-five
long years, did the duke return home again. Of
his life at Blois we know already ; to him and to his
son are chiefly owing those Italian influences which
were most worth copying by French artists, and
which lend their peculiar charm to the work of this
period at Blois. But the most important event
during his life at the castle, both to his family and

to France, was the birth of the young Louis d'Orléans, who was to be King Louis XII. He was held at the font by Louis XI. The father was congratulated by Villon, and by the whole country; and having little else to do in life, he left it gracefully soon afterwards.

The next few years of the story of the Château of Blois are the years of the childhood of the young duke who was to be Louis XII.

With the help of a miniature in a fifteenth-century MS. of the " Roman de Renaud de Montauban," we can imagine the boy seated by his mother at the table beneath a high red canopy upon the dais of the great hall, with two maids of honour in their lofty head-dresses on either side. There is a hound pacing across the tiled floor and watching the pages, who move to and fro between the sideboard and the dais; and from a gallery draped in red, above their heads, the musicians blow quaint instruments and play the tunes that poet Charles delighted in ; while all the time at lower tables the talk flows merrily and unrestrained among the vassals and retainers of the Court.

Saint Gelais tells us how the boy was taught to read before he was seven years old, and soon showed a great love for history, which he probably first read in the four great black velvet volumes of the *Miroir Historial* in his father's library, a kind of unwieldy encyclopædia of the Middle Ages.[1]

[1] The fine library which had been begun by Louis d'Orléans, and

By the age of seventeen he could leap, wrestle, shoot, and play tennis with the best, and particularly aroused the historian's admiration for his excellent horsemanship. Nor was the example of his mother's life thrown away upon him. With the help of her women the good duchess made five hundred shirts yearly to be given away, and quietly provided in many other ways for the poorest inhabitants of every town in which she might be living. She taught her son to be forgiving at any rate, for when he came to the throne after Charles VIII.'s death, he behaved civilly enough to the men who in earlier years had been obliged to oppose him, not only in the Brittany wars but in the haphazard skirmishes in Italy.

" La Trémouille," says Jean Bouchet, " made great mourn at the death of his master King Charles, for with that body he lost all hope of reward for his labours." At Saint Aubin, too, he had soundly beaten Louis, and had little expectation of the generous reception that awaited him at Blois. "Le Roi de France oublie les injures du duc d'Orléans," said the King, and La Trémouille was confirmed in all his states and dignities.

The strength of Louis' character had received a rude shock before this from the unfeeling policy of Louis XI., and he was only enabled to recover at his own accession to the throne. The marriage to Jeanne

which was much improved by Louis XII., was moved by Francis I. to Fontainebleau in 1544.

de France, never one of inclination, must have been very hard for the young prince to bear in the first strength of his manhood.

Our pity for the unhappy victim of her father's cruel calculations has perhaps hardened our judgment upon the young Duke of Orleans.   It is upon Louis XI. that the blame of the inevitable misery that followed should rightly be laid.   Saint Gelais emphasises the impossibility of refusal when once the royal will had been declared, and Jeanne must have long been ready with the gentle words of renunciation and loyalty which La Trémouille brought from her to Louis as soon as Charles VIII. was dead.

Her husband was now King of France, and the necessity for a son to carry on his line was stronger than the ties of individual affection, if indeed we may suppose that Jeanne had ever loved the husband upon whom she had been thrust.   She retired to the Duchy of Berry with a suitable retinue allowed her by the King, and died, with a great reputation for her sanctity of life, in 1504 at Bourges.

The proceedings for divorce had necessitated the presence in France of one whom we have already met at Chinon, Cæsar Borgia, Duc de Valentinois, the bearer of the bull from Alexander VI.

This extraordinary man was a worthy actor of the strange part he had to play, dramatic and inevitable as the succession of events in ancient tragedy. He had come to Chinon bearing besides the bull a

Cardinal's hat for Georges d'Amboise, the first real Cardinal prime minister of France, and in a far more real sense than Balue or Briçonnet, the true forerunner of Richelieu and Mazarin. And now Cæsar's presence at Blois was due to the inevitable return which had to be made for the favour of the Pope's consent. A bride had to be provided for this new prince of France, whose dignities were increased by the gift of the Collar of St. Michael. Frederic of Naples absolutely refused his daughter Carlotta, and the King, after publicly marrying Anne de Bretagne at Nantes in January 1499, proposed Germaine de Foix or Charlotte d'Albret, sister of the King of Navarre, as a wife for the Italian. The latter was selected, and we may hope that, here at any rate, she was happy in a husband who was handsome even for a Borgia ; for his face and figure, we are told, were very near perfection, and he possessed a subtle fascination, even for men, that attracted women as a magnet draws the iron.[1] He wrote to Alexander VI. soon after, describing his impressions of their " mariage de convenance."

---

[1] Of the few portraits left of Cæsar Borgia, Yriarte considers that the woodcut in Paulus Jovius is the most authentic. There is a supposed portrait by Raphael that is not hastily to be accepted. In the Bibliothèque Nationale at Paris there are three types of his face—a woodcut in the style of Albert Dürer, a drawing by Le Cœur which shows a long nose, flowing hair and moustache, and a " bold bad eye," and a cut by B. Bernaerts of Cæsar in youth, with the motto—

" Cui tranquilla quies odio cui proelia cord
Et rixa et caedes seditioque fuit.

See vol. i. p. 63.

No sooner was the wedding over than Louis was
deep in schemes for Italian invasion, which were
certainly as disastrous for France as Lorenzo de
Medicis foretold they would be to Italy. By September in the same year Cæsar himself had gone to
Italy, and his wife was left in France never to see
this strange husband again.[1] With his career in
Italy we have nothing to do. Like a baleful stroke
of lightning he flashed across the clouds of Italian
intrigue, and disappeared before men understood his
meaning.

After his father's death he went to Spain. His
political life was ended, and the epilogue came fitly
in an imprisonment, a wildly venturous escape, and
a death in a skirmish when fighting for the King of
Navarre, against desperate odds, with the rebellious
Comte de Lerins. His memory has been blackened
with the universal condemnation of posterity; but
only to great natures is it given to sin so greatly as
did Cæsar Borgia. Born at a time which had cast
off the old morality and was not yet ready for the
new, he grew up amid the most licentious Court in a

---

[1] Charlotte retired to Valence. Later on she tried to reach her husband in Italy, but he stopped her at Naples : she had become unneces-
sary, and he had no time or inclination for family affection. She then
went to live at Issoudon, a town which had been given to Cæsar, and
there educated her daughter Louise, who in 1516 (two years after her
mother's death) married Louis de la Trémouille. By the treaty of Blois
in October 1505 Germaine de Foix was given to Ferdinand in marriage ;
he was to hand over Naples to her descendants, and cement France and
Spain against the interest of the Borgias.

licentious age; yet, of all who then lived, he alone saw the true issues to which events inevitably tended.

Far differently from his father, the lying, sensual diplomat, he saw, as a true statesman, above all as a thorough soldier, the one end that was worth striving for. While Ludovico Sforza, while the councils of Florence and of Venice were miserably wasting time in weakening their neighbours, he alone saw that the unity of Italy was worth the battle, and was possible, and because he failed he has been pitilessly judged. "Gran conoscitore della occasione," says Machiavelli of this prince, who captivated the intellect of the astute ambassador; and this is his chiefest praise. The friend of Pintoricchio, of Michael Angelo, of Leonardo da Vinci, his engineer, staunch always in his love for Lucrezia—"belle et bonne, douce, courtoise à toutes gens," as Bayard says of her—Cæsar Borgia must be judged, not on his private life, but on his aspirations to his country. He failed, he was crushed by adverse fortune, he died before his youth had grown to the strength that should give fulfilment to its promises; his motto remained, "Aut Cæsar aut nihil." He died too young to be a Cæsar, he was much more than nothing while he lived.[1]

---

[1] The Valentinois title was revived with Diane de Poitiers, and later researches have brought to light that it is still preserved by the Prince of Monaco, as the *Almanach de Gotha* tells us. In the *Standard* for 24th April 1891 occurs the following paragraph : " The last descendant of the once powerful family of Borgias died last week in distressed circumstances. He was the grandson of Don Alberto Calisto di Borgia,

In 1501 a very different scene was passing within the walls of Blois.

Robert de la Marche, who was afterwards the Maréchal de Fleurange, tells us of his introduction to the Court. Being about nine years of age, and "se sentant solide sur son petit cheval, il délibère en lui-même," after the precocious fashion of young adventurers of the time, and at length, with his tutor and some other friends, he rides to Blois to offer the strength of his small arms to King Louis. "Welcome, my son," said the King; "you are too young yet to serve me, and so you shall go live with M. d'Angoulême at Amboise, with whom you will be very happy." —"I will go wherever you may please to order," replied the child. To Amboise he went accordingly, to play with the young Prince Francis, and make friends with the future King of France.[1]

In the same year there was a magnificent reception of the Archduke Philip of Austria at the château. The whole of the State ceremonial has been carefully preserved for us by a conscientious Court chronicler. On the 6th of December the visitors left Orleans

and during the last twenty years had gained his living as a photographer."

[1] As we have seen, Louis XII. died without male issue. Anne de Bretagne had to be content with "ma fille Claude et ma fille Renée." "Anne Reine de France," writes Louise de Savoie, who was watching events eagerly from Amboise, "le jour de Sainte après 21 Jan. eut un fils, mais il ne pouvait retarder l'exaltation de mon César, car il avoit faute de vie."

Louis XII.'s third marriage proved no more fruitful, and Francis, Duc d'Angoulême, became Francis I.

and reached Saint Dié, close to Blois, where
they found several falconers with their birds sent
forward by the King to amuse his guest upon his
way. The Archbishop of Sens, Monsieur de Rohan,
and many others had also come from the Court to
meet him, and all the way along the road the cortège
was met by companies of gentlemen who welcomed
the archduke to Blois. It was late when they all
reached their journey's end, and torches were flashing
from the river as they rode into the town, the ladies
all on palfreys harnessed in black and crimson velvet.
The whole courtyard of the castle was filled with
the King's archers, and the Swiss bodyguards kept
back the crowd that pressed forward to see the procession pass into the doorway of the new-built castle,
that had just been decorated with the porcupine of
Louis XII.

The archduke slowly made his way to the great
hall, which was all hung with cloth of gold, and
tapestry that pictured the fall of Troy. Upon a
broad velvet carpet was the King's chair, with Mon-
seigneur d'Angoulème behind it, and the greetings
were soon over with great courtesy on either side.
The archduchess was some little way behind; the
press had been so great that she was somewhat
separated from her husband, but at last she appeared,
and having obtained the sanction of the Bishop of
Cordova she kissed King Louis and the young duke,
and was then, with great consideration, sent away to

the ladies. . "Madame," said the kindly King, "je sais bien que vous ne demandez qu'à être entre vous femmes, allez vous en voir ma femme, et laissez-nous entre nous hommes." The crowd was still so thick in all the rooms and passages that movement became a thing of time and patience, even for the great ; and when they met the baby princess Claude, carried by Madame de Tournon's daughter, that little lady signified her disapproval of the whole ceremony with such lusty yells that etiquette had to be disregarded, and all the four-and-twenty small girls who followed the princess set themselves loyally to soothe her discontent.

At length the company were distributed in their various rooms, the still-protesting princess to her apartment hung with tapestries of farmyard scenes and "tout petits personnages," the archduke to his chamber, adorned with stories of the Trojan War, and Anne de Bretagne to the room that was decorated with a kind of "natural history pattern" of strange birds and beasts.

Later on refreshments were borne to the archduchess in solemn procession, led by the "maître d'hôtel," with little page-boys after him, clad in yellow silk with velvet slashes, bearing each a waxen candle in a golden candlestick. Madame de Bourbon followed, carrying a great gold box filled with all kinds of confectionery and sweetmeats, then Madame d'Angoulême with a gold box filled with napkins and Madame de Nevers with yet another filled with knives and forks. And so the Court goes pompously to bed, to wake up and find the morning so unkind that the weather barely permitted them to go outside the castle, though the King and the archduke did their best to get sport with their falcons.

Some few more days of solemn ceremony and courtly converse and the guests left Blois in as great state as they came. It is amusing to note with what contempt the chronicler dismisses any attempt at business or State affairs which may have been transacted ; for him it is enough that all the ceremonials were got through decently and in order ; and for us, too, the politics may remain in the background : what little of the history of the times was possible for us has already been described.

It was at this time that the castle began to assume something of its present shape. The whole of the wing in which the entrance door is placed was built and ready for the archduke and his suite. And it is here that we can see Anne de Bretagne at her best, among the ladies of her Court. " Like another Vesta," says Hilarion Costa, "or another Diana, she held all her nymphs in strict discipline, and yet remained full of sweetness and courtesy."

In the library at St. Petersburg there is a picture of the Queen weeping for her husband absent at the wars in Italy. She is dressed in a black head-dress and a square-cut bodice, holding a kerchief to her

eyes and writing. A great bed takes up much of
the room, a bird mopes in a cage, and on the floor
in one corner is a group of girls watching her
silently. In the Bibliothèque Nationale at Paris is the
sequel to the scene. The Queen is now seated upon
a kind of canopied throne, while her women cluster
round admiring the royal letter that is being folded.
Still another picture shows us the Queen, her corded
girdle at her side, and a fine smile of conscious
rectitude upon her face, handing the epistle to her
courier, while the attendant ladies with difficulty
restrain their emotions.

This letter may have been one of those composi-
tions in verse in which Fausto Andrelini assisted, or
Jean d'Auton, the King's historian ; for Anne was
strong in literary tastes, and did much to help her
husband form that famous library, based on the older
collections of his grandfather, which was afterwards
to go to Paris.[1]   One part of the château the Queen
particularly affected.   " Voilà mes Bretons," she would
say, " qui sont sur ma perche et qui m'attendent," and
the terrace where she loved to meet her countrymen
is still known as the " Perche aux Bretons."   These
soldiers were the bodyguard of a hundred gentlemen
whom she had picked out to attend her, in the same
way as she had begun the " Court of ladies," the

[1] Many of the most precious MSS. in the Bibliothèque Nationale
come from this library.
    See Bibl. Nat. MS. No. 5091, in which Jean des Maretz is depicted
giving the Queen a book.

innocent forerunner of the "escadron volant," over which Brantôme waxes so enthusiastic.

On the 9th of January 1514, at the age of thirty-seven years, Anne died at the Château of Blois, to the great grief of her husband. Brantôme has described the magnificence of her funeral.

Not long afterwards Louis XII. followed her to the tomb, and with his death ends the first part of the château's history. He left an ineffaceable mark upon the place, and the porcupines carved here and there upon the walls remind us still of the son of Charles d'Orléans. It was here that he transacted nearly all the important business of the State, the famous Ordonnances of Blois, and the three great treaties of 1504. It was here that he was brought to recover, in his natal air, whenever illness pressed upon him in the more confined atmosphere of the capital.

The love he had for Blois he bequeathed to his daughter Claude, the wife of Francis, to whom is no doubt due the initiation of those magnificent works which were to give a third side to the château, and to provide the background for the drama that is to come, the drama of the sixteenth century that was now well on its way.

CHAPTER XIX

BLOIS (*Continued*)

" Sit subitum quodcunque paras, sit caeca futuri
Mens hominum fati, liceat sperare timenti."
                                          LUCAN.

QUEEN CLAUDE, the daughter of Anne de Bretagne and wife of Francis I., is the link in the history of Blois between the old times and the new. It was her fondness for her father's home that persuaded the King to build the famous wing of Francis I. that was to give shelter after his reign to Marie Stuart, and later on to Henry III.; and at her death it was left unfinished. Francis left it for Gaston d'Orléans to complete in the next century, and went off to build the gigantic Chambord in the plains of the Sologne—Chambord which might have

CLAUDE DE FRANCE, DAUGHTER OF ANNE DE BRETAGNE, WIFE OF FRANCIS I., from the original in the possession of M. Alfred Mame, Tours. Artist unknown, probably Jean Clouet.

Reproduced by permission of M. Péricat, Tours.

been added to the home of Claude, and made of
Blois so fair a palace that Versailles would never
have existed.

For the next few reigns not much of interest
happened at the castle. In 1536 Madame Madeleine
de France was betrothed here to James V. of Scotland, and they were married shortly afterwards in
Paris. A young page went with them, who had
been given to the Scottish King by the Duke of
Orleans, after the fashion of the time: it was
Ronsard, who stayed in the north two years and six
months, and came back at the age of sixteen to go
with De Baïf to Germany, before he settled down in
France as the favourite Court poet of the King.

Of the imitation of classical authors, for which
Michelet so severely criticises Ronsard, there is a
striking example at Blois in 1549, when a " tragedy "
was performed, which was the latest development of
that dramatic instinct which we have already had
occasion to notice.

In the museum now attached to the buildings of
the château there is an old plank covered with rude
paintings and rough verses such as were sung by
the first players of Mysteries and Sottises whom we
found at Amboise. There had been a somewhat
sudden development in these primitive dramatic writings ; the laxity of public morals, and the decline in
public religion which was emphasised by the growing
struggles between Huguenots and Catholics, had

produced their inevitable result in the national literature ; the mystery had been neglected for the farce,
and a strange compromise had been effected between
the two, which by 1541 reached such a pitch of
scandal and disorder that they were definitely suppressed by the Government.   The death of the old
religious theatre was the signal for the rise of the
literary theatre under the auspices of Ronsard and
the Pleiad, and the efforts of these pioneers in the
dramatic art have been somewhat too harshly condemned from a lack of due appreciation of their
strange position.   The old methods had been cast
aside, and for the time no new ones were forthcoming.
It was inevitable that the revival of classical learning,
which was then at its height, should have pointed
out the new way that was to be trodden by the
dramatic author ; so such pieces as *Cléopâtre*, *Médée*,
and *Antigone* appear, mere copies, often bad ones, of
the old originals, but the best then possible.   Not to
every age is it given to produce a Molière, who
should make a national comedy from the old Con-
frères de la Passion at the Hôtel de Bourgogne ;
and this first classical revival which began with
Jodelle and the rest was strong enough to last
through Corneille and Racine, until Dumas and Hugo
startled the literary world with the first French romantic drama, the drama which first drew its scenes from
the history of Touraine, from the "Court of Henry
III." at Blois, and the " Huguenots " at Chenonceaux.

Appropriately enough, it was owing to Catherine
de Medicis that one of these early French adapted
tragedies was played at Blois. Brantôme particularly
praises it, saying that " M. de Saint Gelais composed
it, or rather took and stole it from another, with
better ornamentation." [1]

There were not many fêtes at Blois during the
reign of Henry II., and for the greater part of it
Catherine must bide her time and watch her rival's
triumph at Chenonceaux ; but already the martial
curé at Mériot, who was better at holding pistols
and an arquebuse than at intoning prayers, had discovered the inconveniences of a Church militant
upon earth. Claude Haton's *Mémoires*, full of details
as to weather, crops, and prices, unreliable as records
of character or of policy, are yet full of compassion
for the sufferings of the poor by war and by disease.
They express plainly and simply the common opinions
of the time, and show very fairly the direction in
which affairs were tending. In 1558 he was at Paris
and saw the marriages of Claude de France and
Marie Stuart.

Soon afterwards—

" Pleurez donc la France désolée,'

cry the *Mémoires*,

---

[1] " *Sophonisbe*, tragédie très excellente, tant pour l'agrément que pour
le poly lengage, représentée et prononcée devant le roy, en sa ville de
Blois," Paris, 1559, in 8vo.

"Maudissez le coup de lance,
Maudissez Lorge qui la branle."

Henry II. was dead, and the young King and Queen moved their Court to Blois.

In the new wing of the castle Catherine de Medicis with her two young children, the Duc d'Anjou and Marguerite de Valois, lodged in the rooms that were decorated with the device of Claude, the wife of Francis I., two C's intertwined with lilies and the wings of a swan. The panelling of her library, rescued from the decay into which it had fallen, still shows traces of the colouring which threw into bold relief the exquisite carving of its walls ; there are two hundred and thirty panels here, all different, and each a brilliant example of workmanship and design. This cabinet alone would be sufficient indication of the luxury of decoration lavished by four Valois Courts upon the château ; its solidity is conspicuous in the great wall of division which cuts through the whole wing like a spinal column, and divides each story into a double range of rooms, each large enough, as Balzac said, to hold a company of infantry with ease. Above the rooms of Catherine de Medicis, and with an exactly similar arrangement, were the apartments of Francis II. and Marie Stuart, and it is during their visit here in 1560 that the drama of the Religious Wars, and of the attempts of the Lorraines at power, first began to be unfolded.

EXTERIOR OF THE WEST OF FRANCIS I. AT BLOIS; on the left the Salle des États.

The Guises were at this time in the château, the Duke Francis and the Cardinal ; and though they had, like many others of the Court, their own hotel in the town, they preferred to watch events from close at hand, and were lodged in the rooms of Louis XII. above the twisted columns of the entrance ; and they had many things to watch, for the Loire, then as always, was covered with boats sailing from the west and bearing emissaries from the Huguenot headquarters, or Guisard spies who brought news to the Cardinal ; Catherine herself, " niece of a pope, mother of four Valois, a Queen of France, widow of an ardent enemy of the Huguenots, an Italian Catholic, above all a Medicis," had showed signs of favouring the heretics ; and the Guises were on the alert for traces of conspiracy, eager to crush once and for all the party that opposed them both in religion and in politics. But for the present Catherine seemed inclined to follow her favourite motto, " Odiate e aspettate," and life at the Court went on unwitting of coming change, and happy in the pleasure of the two royal lovers in their rooms above. We can imagine the day on which was first sounded the signal of alarm. The court-yard is filled with officers and men-at-arms, and the sun just rising above the carved and traceried windows of the roof shines on pourpoints and slashed trunk-hose, and glitters on the hilts of swords ; within, all is in the bustle that indicates the

expected presence of the King, who is soon to give
his morning greeting to the Court.   Marshalled under
the watchful eyes of the Comtesse de Fiesque and
the Duchesse de Guise, are the two bands of maids-of-
honour, on one side those of Catherine, on the other
(nearer to the royal apartments) those of Marie
Stuart ; talking to them is the young Prince Charles,
brother of the King, dressed in cloth of gold embroidered with black flowers, and a short black
cloak ; behind him is his tutor Amyot, and farther
on the Chancellor Olivier, while Brantôme has
already begun a conversation with Mademoiselle
de Piennes, one of the maids-of-honour, criticising
the poetry of De Baïf and Du Bellay, who had the
day before arranged a fête for the amusement of the
Court.

Some of the ladies passed the time in reading.
She who was afterwards to be "la belle Fosseuse"
of Henry of Navarre was beginning her education
early with the *Amadis de Gaule*, by the Seigneur
des Essarts ; Madame de Guise fingered Boccaccio's
Celebrated Ladies. Tales of gallantry were at the
time far more in favour at the Court than books upon
religious subjects, or even the many political pamphlets with which the League and its opponents
afterwards flooded the capital and the provinces.

But the Huguenot cause was not without its
representatives even here. Groslot, the servant of
Jeanne d'Albret, was watching the proceedings ;

Coligny and Châtillon are there too, talking with Moret of the visit of Théodore de Bèze to Nérac, when all whisperings ceased suddenly, as Dayelle, the favourite waiting-woman of the Queen, announced that their Majesties were entering the room. The face of Catherine, grave and sombre, almost livid in the daytime though the ivory skin lit up well at night, threw into lively contrast the fresh pink and white of the youthful and piquant Marie Stuart, whose careless gaiety had completely captivated the fragile little King, almost crushed by the severity of his mother.

But on this morning at the Court at Blois all three seemed equally depressed, for strange news had reached them. The Guises, who arranged everything, had suddenly given out that the King's life was in danger, and he must go for safety to Amboise. By degrees the news spread through the ranks of attendant courtiers, to the guards who waited in the embrasures of the staircase, to the men-at-arms below. The assembly in the rooms above broke up hastily, and the château was soon in all the hurry and discomfort of a swift departure.

What passed thereafter at Amboise we know already. It was the beginning of the terrible thirty years of bloodshed that were to be signalised in still more horrible a fashion at the massacre of St. Bartholomew, and were to stain the very walls of

Blois with the traces of their cruelty and their assassinations.   Catherine de Medicis was in her element, the country was full of wars and rumours of wars, and one by one the actors in the drama fall, and their places are taken by others.

Soon after the battle of Dreux, news reached her of the assassination of the Duke of Guise by Poltrot, and she wrote at once to the Cardinal of "le malheureux inconvénient advenu à son frère." Henry, the son of the murdered man, was established in all his father's rights and dignities.

The death of the Prince of Condé, too, brought another Henry on the scene. The young prince of Béarn, who had been placed by his mother, Jeanne d'Albret, under the care of Caumont la Force during the campaign which ended at Jarnac, was now raised to be the head of the Huguenot party, and under the guidance of his mother and Coligny soon made his influence evident to the anxious plotters round the Court of Charles IX.

The position had indeed become one of considerable difficulty, and it was by means of the King's sister, Marguerite de Valois, already famous for her beauty and her wit, that a "rapprochement" was hoped for between the hostile parties.

At Blois the first negotiations were begun by Beauvais, tutor to the young Prince of Navarre, who was sent by Jeanne d'Albret to the Court while she herself went throughout her estates establishing the

reformed religion, strengthening the University of
Béarn, and chasing the Catholic priests out of the
country. Beauvais came back overjoyed with the
reception, but, says Bordenaye, "ceux qui n'avaient
l'entendement opilé par les crudités et viscosités de
l'ambition et de l'avarice avaient ces trop grandes
caresses pour suspectes." Towards the end of 1571
Jeanne d'Albret left her son under the care of Beauvais, and travelled by way of Biron (which she reached
on 21st January in the new year) towards Poitiers,
where the Pope's legate met her coach and passed it
without a sign, for the Queen of Navarre was in no
good odour at the Vatican, and Paul V. had very
vehemently exclaimed against the marriage of a son
of this determined heretic with a Valois princess.
But Charles IX. had expressed his own opinion in
language even more vigorous than the Pope's, and
every preparation was made to receive Jeanne d'Albret
at the Court. The first interview took place at Chenonceaux, but from Tours (which she had only
reached by the 10th of February) the Queen writes
to her son of the difficulties of her position. "Je vous
assure que je suis en grande peine, car l'on me brave
extrêmement et j'ai toutes les patiences du monde."
She sends him news of the Princess Marguerite, and
of her own niece then betrothed to the young Prince
of Condé, with various warnings as to the customs of
the Court ; but it is from Blois that her indignation
really breaks out, at what she sees around her.

Writing from the château on the 8th of March 1572,[1] she complains bitterly of the cynical deceit and carelessness with which her advances are received. " I am so shamefully used," she cries, " that you may well say my patience passes that of Griselda. . . . Madame (Marguerite) is beautiful, witty, and graceful, but brought up in the most terribly corrupted company; there is not one here but is tainted with it. Your cousin, the Marquise, is so changed that there is not a vestige of religion left in her, *save that she never attends mass.* For nothing in the world would I have you living here; there is my reason for your marrying and taking yourself and your wife out of this corruption, for it is far worse than ever I believed. It is no longer the men who ask the women, but the women ask the men. If you were here yourself you would only escape by some remarkable mercy of God. I send you a favour to wear beneath your car since you are now for sale, and some studs for your cap."

Marguerite herself would send no messages to her betrothed, but otherwise was respectful enough to the mother, who admits to Beauvais that the princess

---

[1] The beginning of this now famous letter explains the long time that was taken over the journey. "Mon fils," she writes, "je suis en mal d'enfant, et en telle extrémité que, si je n'eusse pourvu, j'eusse été extrêmement tourmentée." It increases our admiration for her strength of resolution and courage that these difficult negotiations should have been carried on during great bodily distress, and in much mental trouble wilfully caused her by Catherine.

" has a fine figure, but laces herself very tightly, and
uses so much artificial help for her complexion that
I am grieved to think how she will spoil it ; but at
this Court women paint as much as in Spain. You
would scarcely believe how pretty my own daughter
is in these surroundings. Every one attacks her
religion, but she holds her own and gives in not a
whit. Every one loves her."

Coming fresh from her edicts against gaming and
sumptuous apparel in the south, Jeanne d'Albret was
hardly of a mind to appreciate the over-dressed
princess, whom Brantôme describes with so much
enthusiasm at this time, taking part in the procession during the " Pâques Fleuries " at Blois, and re-
splendent in a robe of cloth of gold which had been
given by the Sultan to M. Grandchamp, and by him
presented to Madame Marguerite. " Nor is this all,"
continues the same chronicler, " for she walked in her
place in the procession with her face uncovered, so as
not to deprive men during so great a festival of its
gracious light, and seemed more beautiful still as she
held in her hand her sceptre (as all our Queens wont
to do) with a queenly dignity, with a grace half royal
and half tender."

The fêtes kept up during the whole visit were of
unusual magnificence, and were doubtless meant to
show how much more brilliantly the Catholics could
live than their Protestant opponents. The King was
no unready pupil of his crafty mother, and Coligny

himself had been enticed from La Rochelle to see
the splendour of the Court.[1]

At last the marriage contract was drawn up, and
in June the Queen of Navarre was in Paris.   On the
10th of that month she was dead, being only forty-
four years old.   It may well have been the poisoned
gloves that killed her, as tradition tells, for Maitre
René, Catherine's instrument in such delicate situa-
tions, was equal to gracefully removing any one who
was at all obnoxious to the Queen-mother.

Jeanne d'Albret was too much given to taking
things " au grand sérieux " for this careless and un-
scrupulous age, her religion was too much of a reality
for the polished mockery of Courts, and as like
Coligny she would not bend, like him she must be
broken.   The massacre of St. Bartholomew, in which
the admiral was murdered, took place very shortly
after these events.

Upon the terrace beyond the main building of the
castle is the tower with the letters " Uraniae Sacrum "
inscribed upon its entrance, in which Catherine con-
sulted the stars with her astronomer, and with the

---

[1] There is an interest for Englishmen in the family of Coligny, apart
from the admiration which his character and life must always arouse
among a nation which (whatever its other faults) was certainly averse
to the doubtful methods of policy in favour among Coligny's enemies.
His ancestor was Gaspard de Coligny, Marshal of France under Charles
VIII., Louis XII., and Francis I., and through his uncle, Montmorency, he was connected with the house of Nassau.   William of Nassau
(the Silent) was father of the great General Maurice, grandfather of
Turenne, and great-grandfather of William III. of England.

superstition so common to minds of her peculiar nature, inquired the influence of the planets upon her various schemes. Here she plotted the accession of her son, the Duke of Anjou, to the Crown of Poland, and negotiated, though happily with no success, for his marriage with the English Queen, Elizabeth ;[1] here she dreamed of the carnival of death that was to run riot in the streets of Paris, of the murder of Coligny, of Navarre, of Condé, of all who ever crossed her path—horrors which her son's mind was not strong enough to bear.

In 1574 began the fourth reign in which this woman's sinister influence was to play a part, the reign which brings to its crisis the history of the Château of Blois.

Her son Henry had hurried from Cracow on the death of Charles IX., had gone through the disgusting mockery of penitence in the streets of Avignon, and was beginning his cruel and dissipated career, in which enough of frivolous and exaggerated religion was mingled to rob his carelessness of its one excuse.[2]

---

[1] Elizabeth seems to have been considered a fair mark at this time for all royal matrons with marriageable sons.

There was a scheme afoot at one time to marry her to Henry of Navarre, and join England, France, and Navarre in one great Empire that should recall the dominions of the Angevins. Smith and Throckmorton, the English ambassadors, were in Touraine in 1571, and were spoken to on this strange business.

[2] " Cette vie lâche et méprisable," says Vitet with as much truth as force, " dont une moitié était consacrée aux plus honteuses débauches

There is a small staircase leading from the main buildings of the castle into the great hall in which, in 1576, Henry III. convoked the first States-General of Blois. Henry, the famous Duc de Guise, was at the height of his power ; with the consciousness that Spain was at his back, he was prepared with the League to combat to the full the powers of the King. The famous Catholic League had been thought of so far back as 1562 by the Cardinal de Lorraine at the Council of Trent ; it got its first strength from the Press, and from secret associations in the capital ; indeed, although 1572 had given a bloody proof of its existence, the League, until 1576, remained almost a secret society, with meetings such as that into which the reckless Chicot penetrated and gave Brother Gorenflot so great a reputation for his oratory.

But at this time they felt strong enough to throw off the mask, and the King was fairly terrified at the revelation of the extent of their plans. It must have been a sore surprise for the Guises when the King, in a moment of sudden resolution, declared that he himself would head the famous League ; and we may be sure that all the Court who dared were laughing at the great man's discomfiture.[1]

The King's resolve is described by his sister

et l'autre aux plus ridicules dévotions." The best that can be said for his melancholy culture and refinement is said in Dumas' *Quarante Cinq*, and the rest.

[1] "J'ai détrôné mon cousin de Guise (said Henry to Morvillier), me voilà roi des ligueurs à sa place."

Marguerite, who was present at the meeting of the states of Blois ; and (says her usual ardent admirer Brantôme) the assembly were even more occupied in studying her royal charms than in listening to the excellent discourses of the King. As a matter of fact the King spoke very well and with much dignity when occasion required it, as it did certainly now, for Guise was only put on his mettle by the temporary check, and was soon moving every influence in his power towards his one fixed aim—the King's abasement and his own advance.

D'Aubigné describes how these first estates at Blois dragged wearily on, with demands for redress of grievances [1] alternating with royal complaints of lack of money, and here and there a murder, to diversify proceedings, in the castle grounds. At last the sessions were over, and while, for the sixth time, the Religious Wars began in the South Provinces, within the courtyard of the château the "mignons" of the King, the D'Epernons and Joyeuses of Dumas' famous drama, were swaggering in their short cloaks and long rapiers, and sometimes having serious fights in the midst of the dissipation of the Court.

Thus, Caylus, Maugiron, Livarot, and St. Megrin were beaten by D'Entragues, Schomberg, and Ribeirac, in the famous duel that is immortalised

---

[1] Which had one good result, the "Édit de Blois," a sound measure of reform much needed.

in " La Dame de Montsoreau." The King's grief for his favourites was overwhelming, and he built to their memory a magnificent sepulchre, which was knocked down by the people of the capital soon afterwards. Thus, the Sieur de Saint Sulpice met his death at the hands of the Vicomte de Tours behind the archways in the moonlight, while the courtiers were dancing in the brilliant rooms above, and the King, effeminate enough already, dressed as a woman, was simpering at the jests of the first Italian comedians who had replaced the stormy councillors in the great hall of the castle.

Of the private life of the Court at this time, of the exploits of the " mignons," of Bussy d'Amboise, and the rest, of the King's maudlin affections, his little dogs, his mummeries, his effeminacy, his nauseating mockeries of holiness, the chronicles of the time are full ; and they are not pleasant reading. Small wonder that so many of Montaigne's essays, first printed about 1581, breathe discouragement and weariness of soul at all this purposeless and endless vice and debauchery—this ghastly carelessness of life and of its ending, which is the distinguishing mark of the times of the last Valois.

But even the indolence of the King was at last roused by the startling events that were in progress. On the 1st day of March 1587 L'Estoile chronicles the news of Marie Stuart's execution ; tidings followed fast of the gathering of the Armada that was to be hurled against the English heretics, and the result of the struggle was watched eagerly both by the Guises and the King ; the King, in Chartres, was in fact in deadly fear in spite of his new bodyguard of D'Epernon's Quarante-Cinq, for, contrary to all orders, De Guise had entered Paris, the city had risen in his favour, the very streets been barricaded at the least sign of opposition, and he was actually on his way to demand his appointment as Constable at the coming session of the States at Blois, which the King was unwillingly obliged to summon in October 1588.

Of the three divisions of the Parliament, only in the noblesse could Henry count on a majority, the Guises held the clergy, and the enormous majority of 150 out of 191 in the Tiers État.

The sitting did not promise to be very gratifying to the royal pride, and the King's mind showed traces of irresolution that did not go unmarked by his mother and those who watched him carefully. He had dismissed Cheverny, Villeroi and his old ministers, and taken on Montholon, to every one's surprise, with Ruzé, Révol, and others whom he hoped to influence as he liked. A solemn procession was then started round the town, of all the elected members and the councillors of the Court ; at last the first sitting was definitely fixed for the middle of October. The appearance of the great Salle des États has been often described ; its walls were covered with tapestry, and its pillars twisted with gold lilies upon violet velvet ;

between the third and fourth was placed a dais with
a throne, by which sat the Queen and the Queen-
mother. Strong barriers all round kept the spectators at a distance, and on a chair within them sat
De Guise, in his white satin doublet, watching keenly
all the men of his own party ranged in lines before
him. At last he rose, and mounting the private
staircase to the castle rooms, came back with the
King.

The speech from the Throne was unexpectedly
firm and created a great sensation, but its effect was
somewhat spoilt by Montholon's tedious discussion,
which wandered from Solomon and the Druids to
general exhortations to the assembly, and by the
time the Archbishop of Bourges had mentioned
Nestor and Ulysses, and even dragged in the examples of Nebuchadnezzar and Artaxerxes, the
patience of the house was well-nigh exhausted. The
King's friends had done him little good, and the
Duke of Guise's popularity became more pronounced
than ever; he was proud to excess before, he now
became violent and disrespectful. It was clear to
the anxious King that his conduct was little short of
treasonable; and the jests which the great duke
pitilessly flung to all his followers, about the King
being more fitted for a cloister than a Court, at last
drove Henry's naturally timid and irresolute character
to take a desperate revenge.

Personal enmities have always had much to do

with the crises of French history, and they were not
lacking now to add one more touch to the gloomy
picture whose background was shadowed with the
struggles of fanaticism and persecution, only relieved
by the lurid lights from burning villages throughout
the desolated realm of France.[1]   The Cardinal de
Guise talked of making a crown for Henry with a
dagger's point, and the wicked little Duchesse de
Montpensier, with her pack of cards in her gibecière,
carried on the other side of her girdle the golden
scissors with which she had sworn to cut the tonsure
for the King when he was made a monk.

Anne d'Este was in the Guise's lodgings, the
grand-daughter of Louis XII. and mother of Duke
Henry, who married the Duc de Nemours after her
first husband's death ; his wife, too, Catherine de
Clèves, only left Blois on the 17th of December that
her child might be born at Paris.   His son Charles,
Prince de Joinville, stayed with him all the time, and
spent his days in matches at tennis and flirting with
the maids-of-honour.   All over the castle grounds
the pages of the rival factions were perpetually
quarrelling, and constant duels, in defiance of Court
etiquette, took place in the gardens and the town.

[1] There were horrible cruelties practised on both sides. See the
Theatrum crudelitatum nostri temporis, Anvers, 1587, 4to, where the
Huguenots are represented torturing men and women with cruelties
unspeakable.

The *Oldenburgisches Chronicon,* folio, 1599, shows the reprisals of the
other side—confused scenes of pillage and murder, with Catholic soldiers
sacking the villages of the Huguenots.

At every turn the King saw Guisard faces, watching him and hating him, and every day brought fresh humiliations; like Louis XI., he veiled his projects in a still deeper cloak of exaggerated and loathsome cant and superstition; he even took mass with De Guise on the 4th of December, and on the 18th entered with unusual gaiety into the festivities at the marriage of Christina of Lorraine. The Duke affected to believe the hypocritical expressions of the King, or passed him altogether as beneath contempt, but that very night the murder was first actually spoken of.

Henry's accomplices knew the strength of the man with whom they had to deal; arrangements were made to isolate him from his numerous suite, and a murderer was found courageous enough to strike the blow.

So much ambition and so much contempt could only have one end, but the pride of Le Balafré would only listen to the bolder spirits among his friends; confident in himself and despising his royal enemy, he rejected all the warnings which were showered upon him; a note in his dinner napkin was thrown away unread, and all the vague prophecies with which the air was full were forgotten, or passed over as the idle tales of quacks and prophecy-mongers.

At a supper in the Guises' rooms the position was talked over; the Cardinal and the Archbishop

OPEN STAIRCASE IN THE WING OF FRANCIS I. AT BLOIS.

From a Photograph by M. Péridé, Tours.

of Lyons were there, De Neuilly, Chapelle Marteau, and without doubt the Duchesse de Montpensier in her white damask, with the pink and green embroidery, and her long skirt hiding the slight defect in one leg. The duke's mother, too, was full of anxiety at the constant warnings that reached her.

> " Paris conjure un grand meurtre commettre,
> Blois lui fera sortir son plein effet."

> " La cour sera en un bien fâcheux trouble,
> Le grand de Blois son bon ami tuera,"

were two of the numberless doggerels that every one was quoting at the time. The Duke was again and again besought to beware of Christmas, " for before the year dies you will be dead," had said the prophet.

But as if his destruction had already been fated by a higher power, his usual prudence seemed for the time to have been cast aside, and even the prayers of his mistress, the lovely Charlotte de Sauves, Marquise de Noirmoutier, could not prevail on him either to strike the first blow or to leave the Court that was so full of danger for him, and the town that was notoriously hostile to the League.

Before the breaking of the storm the King kept outwardly very calm, and occupied his leisure in obtrusively pious celebrations of the masses before

Christmas.   On the evening of the 22d the last arrangements were made.[1]

At four o'clock the next morning the King, who had not slept all night, was roused by Du Halde. Several of the Quarante - Cinq were hidden in the staircase leading to the King's "cabinet neuf;" others were disposed in convenient hiding-places along the passages that led from the Council chamber to the royal apartments; others were put in readiness to secure the persons of the Cardinal and the Archbishop of Lyons as soon as the blow had fallen.

The King walked nervously from room to room in the darkness of the December morning, seeing

[1] PLAN OF THE APARTMENTS OF HENRY III. IN FRANCIS I.'S WING AT THE CHÂTEAU OF BLOIS, during the States-General of 1588.
From "Le Château de Blois," par L. de la Saussaye.

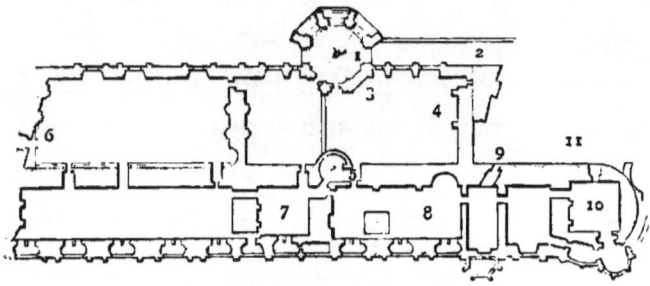

1. The open staircase.
2. Henry II.'s Terrace (leading to Perche aux Bretons).
3. Council Chamber.
4. Fire where Guise was warming himself when the King sent for him. (The arms above the chimney are reproduced on the cover of this book.)
5. Secret staircase (filled with members of the *Quarante-Cinq*).
6. Door leading to the Salle des États.
7. Cabinet Neuf.
8. Bedroom of Henry III. (with position of bed).
9. Passage to Cabinet Vieux.
10. Spot where Guise was first wounded.
11. Cabinet Vieux (since destroyed).

that all was ready, and listening to the chanting of the monks in the alcove hard at hand, who were praying for the success of this cowardly assassination. The members of the Council had been exhorted, the last words of encouragement and warning given to the Quarante - Cinq, swords and daggers even had been served out to those who had none, the ministers were beginning to assemble in the great hall beyond, and still the Duke came not.

De Guise, all unconscious of the imminent peril he was in, had spent the night with the fascinating Madame de Sauves, and only left her at about three in the morning for his own rooms.

It was after eight o'clock when his valets aroused him, saying that the King was on the point of leaving the château, and the Council waited. He walked across the courtyard of the castle to the royal apartments, beneath a dark and threatening sky, "Ce ciel sombre et triste," that was to overshadow the last moments of his life. Upon the terrace La Salle and D'Aubercourt begged him to go back, and he crumpled in his fingers the ninth note of warning since the night.

At the foot of the beautiful staircase,[1] beneath the statues and the twining leaves, is a man-at-arms, the Sieur de Larchant, who entreats the nobleman in

---

[1] Mezeray (iii. 734, fol. 1685) says that Chicot was on the steps, rubbing an old "alumelle" against the window, and murmuring, "Hé j'ay Guise."

power for some favour for the Scottish Guard from
the King himself, and as the Duke ascends, the steps
behind him are closed up with a double file of soldiers,
and all the castle gates are bolted.   A last message
sent him in a handkerchief failed of its purpose, and
in another moment he is in the Council chamber,
pale and cold with the night air, warming himself at
the great fire, eating some plums, and jesting with
the courtiers waiting with him.

The pale face of Révol, the Secretary of State,
just then showed through the open door, and the
message came that His Majesty awaited the Duke
in the Cabinet vieux.   De Guise put some of his
plums in a small box in his pocket, threw the rest
upon the table for the councillors, and with an
" Adieu, messieurs," to them all, left the Council
chamber ; the Sieur de Nambu shut the door
behind him.

The miserable King was not in the room to
which De Guise had been summoned, and which
lay through a narrow passage to the left, but
waiting in the Cabinet de travail at the other end
of his apartments, trembling behind a door until
his cut-throats should have completed their task.

Turning to the left as he came out, the Duke has
reached the end of the room that is crowded with
his murderers, though he knows it not, for he has
bowed to all of them, and gone his way towards the
Cabinet vieux ; there is a pressure on his foot, perhaps

a warning, but it comes too late, and the assassins are close round him.

With a strange feeling of oppression and uncertainty he was half turning back, with one hand on his beard, when he felt the first dagger stroke upon his neck.   It was Montféry who grasped his arm, crying, " Traitor, thou shalt die ! "   At the same time his legs were seized by Des Effranats, Saint Malines stabbed him in the chest, and Loignac thrust him with his rapier through the loins ; but powerful still in his last agony, and with a loud cry for help,[1] he dragged his murderers, struggling, from one end of the room to the other, staggering with arms outstretched, dull eyes within their staring sockets, and mouth half-opened, as one already dead.

At last he fell beside the curtains of the bed. Then came out the King, and with all the meanness of his pitiful nature spurned with his heel the face of the dying man — a terrible reprisal this, for the cruelty of De Guise himself to the gray hairs of Coligny ; and the last sigh of the great duke, who rendered up his strong spirit slowly and with almost unconquerable effort, was received by the courtier who was kneeling down to rifle the pockets of the corpse ; it was covered with a gray cloak, and a cross of straw was thrown upon it.

---

[1] " Le premier coup qu'il reccut luy faisant regorger le sang dans le gosier, il ne put jetter qu'un grand soupir qui fut entendu avec horreur de ceux qui étaient au conseil" (Mezeray, iii. 734, fol. 1685).   For further details see authorities mentioned in the Appendix.

In the confusion that ensued among the crowd in the ante-chamber De Guise's relatives were seized, and the tragedy was completed when his body and that of the murdered Cardinal his brother had been burnt within the castle, and their ashes scattered on the waters of the Loire.

Catherine de Medicis died a few days afterwards, and within a year the King was murdered. The sixteenth century ended red with the blood of its chief actors, and the stage was cleared again for a new reign.

CHAPTER XX

BLOIS (*Concluded*)

"Fy de la Ligue et de son nom,
Fy de la Lorraine estrangère,
Vive le Roi, Vive Bourbon,
Vive la France, nostre mère."

" For the transgressions of a land many are the princes thereof."

WITH the murder of the Balafré the War of the
Three Henrys closed, for now that one was dead, the
other two fell into each other's arms and combined
to crush the party of the League, which still writhed
and tried to sting, although its head was gone.

A meeting between the King and Henry of
Navarre took place at Tours, and their combined
army then moved towards Paris; but Henry III.
was destined never to enter his capital again, and
was stabbed by Jacques Clement at St. Cloud.
With the new reign that begins, the real history
of Touraine is over; the Court is seldom in its
palaces again; but there are still a few more events
which are of interest before the story of the Château
of Blois is done.

After Gabrielle d'Estrées had died and Marguerite de Valois been divorced, Henry IV. brought Marie de Medicis from Italy as his wife. Her magnificent reception and subsequent career are portrayed in the glowing colours of Rubens's great series of complimentary historical pictures ; but the connection of Marie with the Castle of Blois was only of the most humiliating description.

The Vert Galant had been stabbed by Ravaillac in the very midst of his pursuit of the lovely Princess of Condé, in the course of which he had threatened to set all Europe by the ears for the sake of one woman, as Buckingham was to do after him ; and during the reign of the next King, the sombre

STATUETTE FROM THE OPEN STAIRCASE AT THE CHÂTEAU OF BLOIS; see p. 117. (The figure to the right of the entrance.)

Medicean Louis XIII., the position of the Queen-mother had become one of very considerable difficulty. Her embarrassments, political and otherwise,

at last landed her in the Château of Blois, and there
the King's favourite, De Luynes, showed every intention of keeping her shut up and out of harm's
way. The tortuous designs of Richelieu, who had
accompanied her, were not yet clear; and he was
ordered to leave her household and retire to Avignon.
The position of Marie de Medicis became more and
more intolerable, for De Roissy, the governor of the
castle, seemed to take pleasure in making her captivity as odious as possible. De Luynes set his mind
at rest, and proceeded with his own affairs at Paris,
confident that the Queen-mother would trouble him
no more. But the numerous political executions,
which were at this time constantly taking place,
so roused the indignation of the people, that the
nobles resolved to take advantage of the crisis and
liberate the Queen-mother.

The Dukes of Rohan and Montbazon resolved to
effect a reconciliation between the King and Marie
de Medicis at all costs. Her friends the Concinis
were working for the royal captive, and they had
sent the Abbé Ruccelai to manage her escape from
Blois. That this was no easy matter is shown by the
fact that it took two years to make the necessary
preparations. On 22d January 1619 D'Epernon left
Metz with a hundred well-armed men, his guards and
personal attendants, his jewels, and eight thousand
pistoles. His letters to the Queen were carried by
treachery to De Luynes, who fortunately disregarded

them, and after much uneasiness Marie heard at last that D'Epernon was at Loches, where a refuge had been arranged for her.

On the 21st of February 1619 a certain Cadillac was walking at midnight across the bridge, when he met some of the Queen's friends who had been sent out to say that all was ready. They all went to the foot of the wall in which her window opened, where much agitated talking could be heard. After great hesitation the Comte de Brienne appeared down a rope-ladder, and Marie de Medicis after him, in an attitude more calculated for safety than for that dignity with which she had been portrayed by Rubens. One ladder was enough for the poor Queen, who had had great difficulty in getting through the window, and was accompanied by only a single waiting-woman ; the rest of the descent from the platform to the ditch of the castle was made upon a cloak spread out upon the slope. Friends were waiting at the bottom, and walked her quickly off, one upon each side ; but no carriage was to be seen. After a moment of intense anxiety it was found hiding in a side street ; then the royal jewels had been forgotten. More suspense till they were recovered, dropped in the haste of escaping, beneath the castle walls. At last the carriage started, and Marie de Medicis was free to begin plotting again with her clumsy Gaston against the astute and omni-potent Richelieu.

Gaston had neither the skill to foil him nor the courage to assassinate him, and no Aramis or Porthos was at hand to help, for Monsieur d'Orléans had an evil notoriety for abandoning his friends to their fate without lifting a finger to save them ; so he failed as he was bound to do, and found himself sent into exile, after the Fronde had given the final death-blow to his schemes, to the Château of Blois.

Here, in 1635, he was living with his solemn Court ; and Mademoiselle de Montpensier his daughter, " La grande Mademoiselle," as she was called, gives a pitilessly accurate account of the wearisome etiquette of the Duke of Orleans' household. " Monsieur dissertoit, distinguoit, Hésitoit comme à l'ordinaire." [1] After both the King and Queen had followed Richelieu to the tomb, the unlucky Gaston heard once more the shouts of " Vive le Roi ! " which had grown so distasteful to his envious ears, and the quiet of his Court was interrupted by the visit of the young King Louis.

At the end of April 1644 John Evelyn had come down the Loire by boat from Orleans to Blois, and his diary is worth quoting to describe for us the state of the château at this time. They arrived in the evening, and noticed the " stately stone bridge on which is a pyramid with an inscription. At the entrance of the castle," he continues, " is a stone

---

[1] Compare De Retz : " Monsieur n'agissait jamais que quand il était pressé, et Frémont l'appelait ' *l'interlocutaire incarné.* ' "

statue of Lewis XII. on horseback as large as life,
under a Gothic state.[1] Under this is a very wide
payre of gates nailed full of wolves and wild boars'
heads. Behind the castle the present Duke Gastion
(*sic*) had begun a faire building through which we
walked into a large garden, esteemed for its furniture
one of the fairest, especially for simples and exotic
plants, in which he takes extraordinary delight. On
the right hand is a long gallery, full of ancient statues
and inscriptions, both of marble and brasse ; the
length, 300 paces, divides the garden into higher
and lower grounds, having a very noble fountain.
. . . From hence we proceeded with a friend of mine
through the adjoining forest to see if we could meete
any wolves, which are here in such numbers that they
often come and take children out of the very streetes ;
yet will not the duke, who is sov'raigne here, permite
them to be destroyed. . . . Bloys is a town where
the language is exactly spoken ; the inhabitants very
courteous ; the ayre so good, that it is the ordinary
nursery of the King's children."

Evelyn came too soon to see the streets of
the town decorated for the entry of the young
King Louis XIV., the great State carriages, huge
machines of wood and leather with enormous nails,

[1] This is the statue that was destroyed in the Revolution. The old
inscription ran—

"Hic ubi natus erat dextro Ludovicus Olympo
Sumpsit honorata regia sceptra manu ;
Felix quae tanti fulsit lux nuncia Regis
Gallica non alio principe digna fuit."

Genoa velvet curtains and wide wheels ; to watch the
musketeers in their brilliant uniform, the light blue
cosaque with a great star on breast and back, the
long-plumed hat, and high soft boots to the knee.
The gay procession goes laughing on to the castle,
and from the windows in the court above us, which
had just been filled with the terrible shadows of the
murdered Guises, it was a relief to hear the whispers
of that roguish Montalais as she pointed out the young
Vicomte de Bragelonne to Louise de la Vallière.
Mazarin was adding up accounts in his bedroom on
the other side, and the exiled English King was asking D'Artagnan the way to Louis XIV.'s apartments.

But the visit did not last long. Mademoiselle
tells us the Court were bored to death, as well they
might be ; and the King was soon away to meet his
Spanish bride, without a thought that the young
maid-of-honour he had seen at Blois was one day to
hold so tender a place in his impressionable royal
heart.

This was the last of the splendour of Blois.
Gaston returned to his solemnity and his gardening,
and after his death in 1660 the whole place was
dismantled.

Arthur Young, passing it in 1787, could still be
shown the details of the Guises' murder, and his
eminently practical reflections thereupon are worth
transcribing. "The character of the period," says
he, "and of the men that figured in it, were alike

disgusting.   Bigotry and ambition equally dark, in-
sidious, and bloody, allow no feelings of regret.   The
parties could hardly be better employed than in
cutting each other's throats."   So far our honest
agriculturist, who happily finds much soil suited to
his taste farther on in the Sologne plains, and leaves
Blois to be still further defaced by the Revolution
which followed hard upon this peaceful visit.

In the terrible devastations of 1793 Blois suffered
like the rest for its royal recollections, and was as
usual converted into barracks ; in 1871 it served as
an ambulance for the wounded in the Franco-Prussian
war ; and finally it is restored to-day with an abundance of care and thought worthy of the structure
which holds so many memories.   The rooms are
even too vividly restored, as we have noticed, with
brilliant colourings on ceiling and on floor, and gor-
geous tapestries on all the walls ; but they only need
kindly time to soften them again, and they are
peopled for ever with the shadows of their history.

But much as there is for the traveller to see in
the great Château of Blois, he must by no means
leave the town with only the royal palace explored.
He will find numerous churches all well worth his
visiting ; he will see, most beautiful of all, the Hôtel
d'Alluye, where Florimond Robertet, the famous
secretary, lived, and from the gardens that slope
downwards to the river he will see the other bank of
the stream, the country of the Sologne, and the bridge

that points him on to Chambord, where Porthos, kindly giant, might have found a home, when Bracieux close by became too small for him.

The history with which these pages have had too hastily to deal is now brought to its farthest point. From château to château we have followed it till the chain that began with the Plantagenets at Chinon is

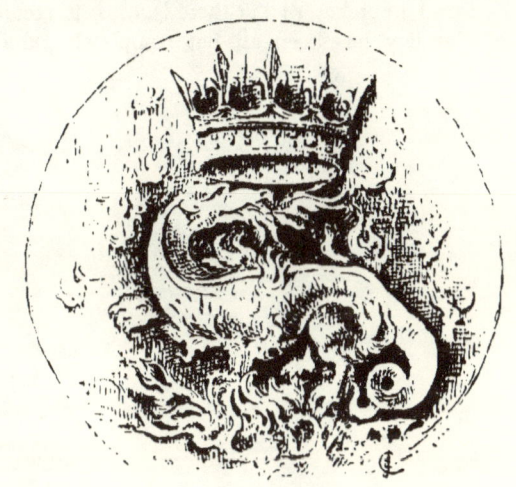

SALAMANDER FROM THE WALLS OF THE CHÂTEAU OF BLOIS
(the badge of Francis I.)

broken with the murder of the Balafré at Blois. The seventeenth century is the century of the intrigues of Paris, the age of Versailles and Fontainebleau, and Touraine is all but neglected by the Court. Yet it is impossible to leave Touraine without visiting the gigantic Chambord, without glancing, though but for a moment, at a few more of the noble houses scattered through the province, without finishing the brief sketch of the central town of Tours which was begun earlier in this book.

These last things, then, we have left to do, and then bid the traveller wander at his will.[1]

---

[1] Nearly all the notes from which the foregoing chapters were written were taken during the summer and autumn of 1890. A few changes noticed on a short visit in 1891 will be found in the Appendix. At the present moment (December 1891) I hear that Chenonceaux has at last actually found a purchaser; but there is a loss to record as well; the Abbey of Cormery has been all but completely ruined by the storms.

CHAPTER XXI

CHAMBORD

" Ledict bastiment estoit cent fois plus magnifique que n'est Bonivet ne Chambourg ne Chantilly : car en icellui estoient neuf mille trois cents trente et deux chambres, chascune garnie de arrière chambre, cabinet, garderobe, chapelle, et issue en une grande salle."—La vie très horrifique du grand Gargantua, cap. liii.

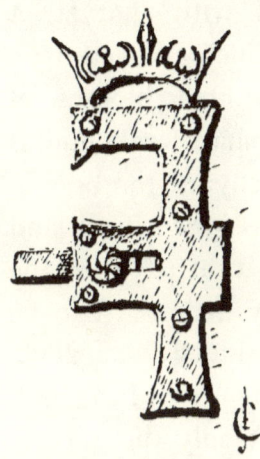

IRONWORK LOCK FROM CHAM-BORD, THE CROWNED F OF FRANCIS I.

(From the Collection of M Lacoste, Rue des Saints Pères, Paris)

THE road that leads from Blois to Chambord crosses the Loire by a fine stone bridge, which the inscription sets forth to be the first public work of Louis Philippe.

For some distance the rails of a small tramway followed the road by which our carriage was slowly rolling towards the level plains of the Sologne, but we gradually left such uncompromising signs of activity, and came into a flat country of endless vineyards, with here and there a small plaster tower showing its slated roof above

the low green clusters of the vines.[1] We passed
through several villages, whose inhabitants that day
seemed to have but one care upon their minds, like
the famous Scilly Islanders, to gain a precarious
livelihood by taking in each other's washing.   On
every bush and briar fluttered the household linen
and the family apparel, of various textures and in
different states of disrepair ; and with that strict
observance of utility which is the chief characteristic
of the French peasant, the inevitable blouses of
faded blue were being blown into shapeless bundles
even along the railings of the churchyard tombs.

At last we came to an old moss-grown wall, and
through a broken gateway entered what is called the
Park of Chambord.   There is very little of it to be
seen now, the trees have been ruthlessly cut down
and mutilated, and of the wild boars which Francis I.
was so fond of hunting there is left only the ghostly
quarry that Thibault of Champagne chases through
the air, while the sound of his ghostly horn echoes
down the autumn night as the phantom pack sweeps
by to Montfrault.[2]

---

[1] These towers may very possibly be modern erections connected
with the cultivation of these enormous and apparently uninhabited
regions, but they are very like the old watch-towers which M. Prosper
Mérimée reproduces from a fifteenth-century MS., showing the beacons
that flamed from its roof, while watchdogs beneath are couched behind
an encircling hedge of wattles.

[2] Called in the country the "Chasse du comte Thibault" (le Tricheur),
or the "Chasse Machabée."   Touraine has also its "danse macabre," the
"chasse du roi Hugon."   In Poitou there is the "chasse Galerie," with

The woods that inspired such graceful reflections in Pelisson's letter to Mademoiselle de Scudéry (1668) have little left of the romantic now ; indeed when Arthur Young drove through them a century ago the only reflections they suggest to him are "that if the King of France ever formed the idea of establishing one compleat and perfect farm under the turnip culture of England, here is the place for it." And Paul Louis Courier would have thoroughly agreed with him.

At the end of a sufficiently long avenue, the very ghost of an avenue, which only showed more desolation upon either hand as it advanced, could be seen at last what seemed a village in the air. Gradually the village showed its foundations on the solid earth, and we were soon beneath the shadow of the enormous towers of Chambord, towers of immense girth yet with a somewhat squat expression, which we found out afterwards was the result of the disproportionate elaboration of the upper parts of the building. There are thirteen great staircases in this wilderness of hewn stone, not to mention the number-less smaller ones, and four hundred and more rooms of various sizes : the resulting impression, though we were spared from seeing more than about a quarter, was that of a vast and comfortless barrack, and as all its sixteenth-century art treasures had perished

many other examples for the comparative mythologist of the widespread story of the Spectre Huntsman.

with the rest of the furniture and fittings in the
vast bonfire of the Revolution, the great empty
rooms had even less chance than was perhaps fair
of showing how far their size was equalled by their
comfort.

It is impossible for the uninstructed mind to
grasp the plan or method of this mass of architecture ; yet it is unsatisfactory to give it up, with
Mr. Henry James, "as an irresponsible, insoluble
labyrinth." M. Viollet le Duc, with a sympathetic
denial of any extreme and over-technical admiration,
gives just that intelligible account of the château
which is a compromise between the unmeaning
adulation of its contemporary critics and the ignorance of the casual traveller.

"Chambord," says he, "must be taken for what
it is ; for an attempt in which the architect has sought
to reconcile the methods of two opposite principles,
to unite in one building the fortified castle of the
Middle Ages and the pleasure-palace" of the sixteenth century. Granted that the attempt was an
absurd one, it must be remembered that the Renaissance was but just beginning in France ; Gothic art
seemed out of date, yet none other had established
itself to take its place. In literature, in morals, as
in architecture, this particular phase in the civilisation
of the time has already become evident even in the
course of these small wanderings in a single province,
and if only this transition period is realised in all

its meaning, with all the "monstrous and inform" characteristics that were inevitably a part of it, the mystery of this strange sixteenth century in France is half explained, of this "glorious devil, large in

Drawing (from Viollet le Duc) to illustrate the transition in architecture in a tower at Chambord. On the left is an old feudal tower, with an opening cut down the middle (showing the various floors), on the right a window is being fitted into the opening, and to hide the join of the old masonry with the new, light pilasters are run up the sides, the origin of the Renaissance window.

heart and brain, That did love beauty only," and would have it somewhere, somehow, at whatever cost.

Francis I. had passed his early years at Cognac, at Amboise, or Romorantin, and when he first saw Chambord it was only the old feudal manor-house built by the Counts of Blois. He transformed it, not by the help of Primaticcio, with whose name it is tempting to associate any building of this King's, for the methods of contemporary Italian architecture were totally different; but, as M. de la Saussaye proves, by the skill of that fertile school of art and architecture round Tours and Blois, and more particularly of one Maître Pierre Trinqueau, or Le Nepveu, whose name is connected with more successful buildings at Amboise and Blois. The plan is that of the true French château ; in the centre is the habitation of the seigneur and his family, flanked by four angle towers ; on three sides is a court closed by buildings, also with towers at each angle, and like most feudal dwellings the central donjon has one of its sides on the exterior of the whole.

Though all ideas of a practical defence are sacrificed to produce a dwelling-house, yet this house is furnished with secret stairways, with isolated turrets, with numberless facilities for what the gallant M. Viollet le Duc calls " les intrigues secrètes de cette cour jeune et toute occupée de galanteries," which kept up the constant semblance of a mimic war. Michelet, romantic as ever, explains the strangeness of the plan of Chambord by the state of mind in which the grandson of Valentine Visconti returned

from his prison at Madrid ; but the château of Long-
champs with the exquisite work of Girolamo della
Robbia, which was begun only a year after (1527),
seems sufficient contradiction, if that were necessary,
to this last theory.

It may well be imagined that Chambord is the

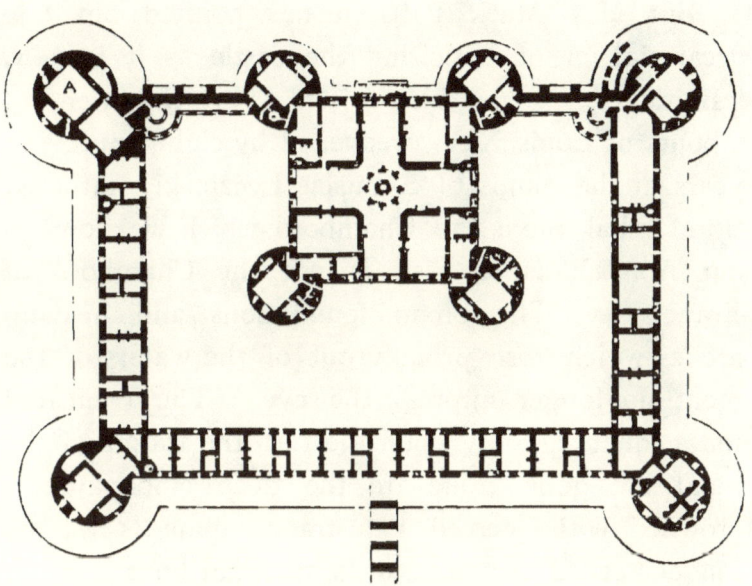

PLAN OF THE CHÂTEAU OF CHAMBORD (à l'échelle d'un demi-millimètre pour
mètre.—*Viollet le Duc*).

parody of the old feudal castles, just as the Abbey
of Thelema parodies the abbeys of the twelfth and
thirteenth centuries. Both heaped a fatal ridicule
upon the bygone age, but what Rabelais could only
dream Francis could realise, yet not with the unfettered perfection that was granted to the vision of
Gargantua ; for surely never was the spirit of the time

seized and smitten into incongruous shapes of stone at so unfortunate a moment, just when the early Renaissance was striving to take upon itself the burden which was too heavy for the failing Gothic spirit, just when success was coming but had not yet come.

But Mrs. Mark Pattison has pointed out one great danger of criticising the castle as it is now. "Burdened," says this writer,[1] "by the weighty labours of Louis XIV., weakened by eight improving years at the hands of Stanislas Leczinski, mutilated by Marshal Saxe, the Chambord which we now go out from Blois to visit is not the Chambord of Francis I. The broad foundations and heaving arches which rose proudly out of the waters of the moat no longer impress the eye. The truncated mass squats ignobly upon the turf, the waters of the moat are gone, gone are the deep embankments crowned with pierced balustrades, gone is the no longer needed bridge with its guardian lions."

It is only from within the court, where the great towers fling their shadows over the space, where pinnacles and gables soar into the air, and strange gargoyles and projections shoot from the darkness into light, that it is possible to realise the admiration which Chambord roused when it was first created. Brantôme waxes enthusiastic over its wonders, and describes how the King had drawn up plans

---

[1] *Renaissance of Art in France*, vol. i. 55.

VIEW OF THE CHÂTEAU OF CHAMBORD, from an old print in *Vues des Belles Maisons des Environs de Paris* (now in the Library of Wadham College, Oxford).

(mercifully never carried out) to divert the waters of the Loire to his new palace, not content with the slender stream of Cosson, from which the place derived its name.[1]   Others compare it to a palace out of the *Arabian Nights* raised at the prince's bidding by a genie, or like Lippomano, the Venetian ambassador, to "the abode of Morgana or Alcinous"; but this topheavy barrack is anything rather than a "monument féerique"; it might with as much humour be called a "souvenir de premières amours," as the learned M. de la Saussaye has it.   Both these descriptions fit Chenonceaux admirably; when used of Chambord they are out of place.

The praises of contemporary critics may have been more genuine when they drew attention to the marvellous staircase in the middle of the château, which is the first thing to which the guide directs his visitors.   This is indeed a gigantic freak of fancy, and worthy of the buildings which contain it, where Gargantua and Pantagruel might have wandered amid congenial surroundings.

It has two openings, and by imagining two huge corkscrews one within the other, whose curves ascend together yet never touch except at their extreme

---

[1] Chambord is apparently the correct spelling, not Cham*bourg*; from which it would seem that the name is derived from the Celtic "cam" (French *courbe*), from the turn which the Cosson takes at this point, and "rhyd," a ford or passage.

Cf. "*Cam*bridge"=the passage over the twisting river.—M. de la Saussaye, *Chambord*, p. 44.

edges, the perplexed visitor strives to understand how it comes about that his companion, who is mounting upward like himself, can never meet him though never be completely lost.

From the country visible from the open top of this staircase, one of the chief ornaments of the roof, it is perhaps possible to assign a reason for the position of the old castle, which is confirmed by a manuscript in the library of Blois. The place seems originally to have formed part of a system which guarded the approaches of the Loire, and made it possible for Joan of Arc to move up the river to Orleans. This old fortress of the Counts of Blois and Champagne passed with the rest of the estates to the family of the Dukes of Orleans, and through them to the Crown, at the accession of Louis XII.; this it was that his successor Francis changed into an unwieldy hunting-seat in 1526. For twelve years eighteen hundred workmen laboured incessantly at the task, and it was handed on to the next reign unfinished.

Here came Francis towards the end of his life, when he sought vainly to forget the fever that was in him by wild hunting excursions throughout his great estates in Touraine, and with him his sister, the Queen of Navarre, his "rare pale Margaret," whose eyes, "ever trembling through the dew of dainty woful sympathies," were anxiously watching her idolised brother in his sickness. It was in one of their conversations that Francis, perhaps grown wiser with experience, echoed Virgil with his lines upon the fickleness of woman. Tradition says that the pane of glass which so ungallantly preserved the words—

> " Toute femme varie
> Mal habil qui s'y fie,"

was broken by a later King whose philosophy was not yet proof to the fascinations of Louise de la Vallière.[1]

Charles IX. came here after Francis I. had gone to hunt shadowy boars in the Elysian fields, but there was not much happening at the castle for the next few reigns. Henry IV. found himself far too busy to leave Paris, and too happy at Fontainebleau with Gabrielle d'Estrées, who probably found Chenonceaux far more to her taste when she went excursions into the country.

Later on, Louis XIII. was wandering in his melancholy way through the corridors of Chambord, with his arm in that of his favourite for the time being.

---

[1] There has been much controversy about this famous inscription. Even the phrasing of it differs in every authority, especially for the second line. There are three proofs from which I have argued its existence. (1) The statement in the *Lettres Inédites de la Reine Marguerite*, Partie 1re ; (2) the testimony of Brantôme, an eye-witness, "et l'ayant leu en grande lettre, y avoit ce mot : Toute femme varie" (*Brantôme*, ed. Lalanne, t. ix. p. 715) ; (3) in 1682 Bernier (*Histoire de Blois*, p. 8) says "l'on y voit cette rime," etc. Whether it was Louis XIV. or not who destroyed it, it exists no longer ; and even the signature which M. de la Saussaye considers to be that of Francis is totally unlike his handwriting in the MSS. of the Bibliothèque Nationale. See pp. 211 (vol. i.), 140 (vol. ii.)

"Mettons nous à cette fenêtre, Monsieur," he was saying, "et ennuyons nous"—apparently this was the one occupation of a monarch who was more thoroughly bored with himself and others than any crowned head in Europe. "Vexed with a morbid devil in his blood, That veiled the world with jaundice," his very love affairs were so morosely platonic that the Court almost lost interest in their incidents. It was at Chambord that this timid lover, wishing to take a note from the fair Mademoiselle de Hautefort, who had hidden it in her bosom, advanced to capture the missive with a pair of tongs.[1] His father could have taught him better manners, more gallantry or less of clumsiness.

In the fourth act of Victor Hugo's drama we can see the curtain lifted for a moment upon the Court at Chambord. There is the King, who finds it hard enough to live, without the added trouble of a

---

[1] The science of correct dates will very soon make any romance in history impossible. It is argued that because the lady was born in 1616, and Chambord was given to Prince Gaston in 1626, this incident did not occur. Tallemant des Réaux, whom Dumas considers a sufficient authority, relates it ; and why should it not have been at Chambord, where tradition insists that the event took place, and where the courtiers who laughed over the *Bourgeois Gentilhomme* were still told the story that had lasted to their days in all its piquancy? The place where Mademoiselle de Hautefort hid the innocent epistle had achieved a certain amount of reputation in French literature ; Boisrobert writes of a pearl that was equally fortunate—

> " Ne te plains pas du piège où je te vois tombée,
> Riche perle qui fais le plaisir de nos yeux :
> La gorge qui t'a dérobée
> Fait des larcins plus precieux !"

kingdom, striving to shake off the power of Richelieu, whose scarlet robes so terribly suggest the powers of his office. " La pourpre est faite avec des gouttes de leur sang." There is the Duc de Bellegarde, laughing with the Marquis de Nangis, while a Mousquetaire stands sentinel before the royal door ; De Retz is here too, and L'Angely the jester, and the Vicomte de Rohan, who makes a strange discovery behind the arras, for Marion de Lorme is there, pleading in terrible earnest for her lover's life.

It was not often that so interesting a "scene " took place at Chambord. When in 1626 the castle became the property of Monsieur Gaston, brother of the King, the small Mademoiselle de Montpensier found much innocent amusement in laughing up and down the winding steps of that perplexing staircase, while her solemn father mounted with her to the open lantern at the top. Gaston, with his red beard and sleepy eyes, was probably as mystified as his more lively daughter ; but Gaston seldom laughed, and would never admit his perspicuity to be at fault. It would have been fortunate for him, perhaps, if the problem of that staircase had been the only one his dull brains had tried to fathom, or if he had kept to his botanical researches with his physician, Albert Brunyer. His attempts at politics only revealed, by the dastardly abandonment of Chalais, of Cinq Mars, and De Thou, that to his general faults of ignorance and incapacity must be added the severer blame of an unpardonable ingratitude.[1]

But with nothing save a staircase to recommend it by way of frivolous amusement, it is easily intelligible that Chambord was no favourite with the Dianes and Gabrielles of the period ; and Madame de Maintenon, at a time when Louis XIV. gave the place one of its few glimpses of royal gaiety, seems to have spent her time there chiefly in quarrelling with Madame de Montespan. It was in one of the great rooms on which the staircase opens that Louis XIV. sat, solemn and bored, amid a sympathetically jaded Court to hear the first performance of *Pourceaugnac.* Molière was ill, and Lulli, who had on the instant filled the vacant place, was in despair at the array of long-drawn faces listening wearily before the stage. Something must be done to rouse the King. Our courageous Lulli suddenly bounds across the footlights, and from the débris of a discomfited orchestra joyfully detects the peal of royal laughter that greets this unexpected piece of acting. The play ended in a general applause. *Le Bourgeois Gentilhomme* was more successful, and at once, as it deserved to be. It is amusing to detect the satisfaction of M. l'Ambassadeur from the Levant, who

---

[1] "Monsieur," says that acute observer, De Retz, "était un des hommes du monde le plus faible, et tout ensemble le plus défiant et le plus couvert . . . il faisait en toutes choses comme font la plupart des hommes quand ils se baignent : ils ferment les yeux en se jetant dans l'eau."

takes to himself all the credit of the Turkish meta-
morphosis and superintends the correct Eastern
costume and *mise-en-scène* for M. Molière.

In 1725 the luckless Stanislas Leczinski found a
home here, to mourn over his lost Poland, and left an
appropriate memory of kindliness and charity among
the scattered peasantry of the neighbourhood.

The next tenant was of a very different character.
The astonished villagers could now hear words of command echoing from the terrace, and see squadrons of
horse wheeling to and fro under the orders of the
conqueror of Fontenoy.

Maurice de Saxe, the newcomer, owed his birth
to a strange and still unexplained event. In 1695
Sophia Dorothea, wife of the Electoral Prince of
Hanover, was sent suddenly to prison in the fortress
of Ahlden, and her lover, Count Philip von Konigsmarck, simultaneously disappeared. His sister,
Aurora von Konigsmarck, went to seek help from
Augustus the Strong, Elector of Saxony, and the
negotiations resulted in the birth of Marshal Saxe.
After a rough education, he went to France and
waited for a chance of fighting, consoling himself in
the interval with Adrienne Lecouvreur. He was six
feet high, with good features, blue eyes, and black
arched brows, and needed only the address which
every Konigsmarck possessed to prove himself capable of procuring " consolation " whenever he might
need to seek it.

At last, in 1740, came the league against Maria Theresa ; and five years afterwards, though he had just been tapped for dropsy and was carried in a litter on the field, chewing a bullet to ease his raging thirst, he had defeated Cumberland at Fontenoy and opened the way to the Scheldt. He was rewarded with the estate of Chambord, which he forthwith decorated with his captured cannon and filled with his bodyguard of Uhlans, and then proceeded to forget as fast as possible the politics which had given him his chance of victory. " I know nothing about your infernal reasons of state," he cried to the Comte de Maurepas, and at once began to thoroughly enjoy himself after his own manner.[1]

Fêtes and reviews, such as had not been seen since the building of the château, were now the order of the day ; and the Marshal would soon have killed himself off in the ordinary course of events, had not an old enemy appeared to save him the trouble. A letter was suddenly brought one morning from a carriage that had just driven through the park. Marshal Saxe at once went out, attended only by an aide-de-camp, and disappeared in one of the alleys branching out into the forest from the main drive. In a short time he was carried home badly wounded.

---

[1] By an actress, Mademoiselle Verières, he had a daughter Aurora who married a M. Dupin de Francueil, and became the mother of George Sand, whom we have heard of already at Chenonceaux.

There had been a duel with the Prince of Conti, who had been his enemy ever since the Flanders campaign of 1747, and the Marshal had been worsted.

The doctors could do nothing for him, and like Rabelais he went with a laugh to seek the "grand peut-être." " Life," said the dying general, " is but a dream. Mine has been short, but it has been a good one."

It is strange that almost the only bit of the old furniture left by the Revolution was the great marble table on which the body of Marshal Saxe had been embalmed. This same outburst of revolutionary iconoclasts came very near pulling down Chambord altogether, which at any rate deserved to remain when once it had been built ; and after refusing to sell it to a society of Quakers, who hoped to make use of it no doubt in some pacific schemes of manufacture, they pulled down all the fleurs - de - lys within reach and otherwise mutilated the place, according to the Republican standard. And when Madame la Duchesse de Berry visited it in 1828, she must have been astonished to find the disorder which a few regiments with a proper spirit can effect in the strongest Royalist abode.

Chambord was at this time the property of Henri de Bourbon, who, though he was in exile, took his title from this estate in France, which had been presented to him by national subscription. The subscription itself is chiefly memorable for the brilliant

pamphlet which it evoked from Paul Louis Courier,
the "Simple Discours du Vigneron de la Chavon-
nière."[1]

In 1870 Chambord was garrisoned in earnest by
the French, who were as usual taken by surprise by
a German attack and compelled to make a strategic
movement to the rear.   In the next year the Comte
de Chambord wrote the famous letter about the
white flag of the Bourbons, on one of the few visits
he ever made to the estate.   "This amazing epistle,"
says Mr. Henry James, "which is virtually an in-
vitation to the French people to repudiate as their
national ensign that immortal tricolour, the flag of
the Revolution and the Empire, under which they
have won the glory which of all glories has hitherto
been dearest to them. . . . This luckless manifesto,
I say, appears to give the measure of the political
wisdom of Henry V.   It is the most factitious
proposal ever addressed to an eminently ironical
nation."

The Prince's rooms, decorated with the most
impossible of tapestries presented by the ladies of
France, are exhibited by the guide, and his vast
collection of extremely military toys of great perfection of workmanship and detail.   There is also

---

[1] The pamphlet begins : "Si nous avions de l'argent à n'en savoir
que faire, toutes nos dettes payées, nos chemins réparés . . . je crois,
mes amis, qu'il faudrait contribuer à refaire le pont de Saint Avertin
. . . mais d'acheter Chambord pour le duc de Bordeaux je ne suis pas
d'avis."

here an excellent statue of the Madame Elizabeth who so courageously attempted to save the Queen, and at the last died with her. It is one more memento among many, of the terrible effects of the Revolution.

Our last, and perhaps most satisfactory, visit was to the forest of masonry upon the roof. Chimneys had expanded into monuments and lanterns into mausoleums, yet none of the grace with which the chimneys are treated at Azay or Chenonceaux is visible ; nothing strikes the onlooker but a massiveness without much object, in which any beauty of detail [1] is only thrown away.

Only as we began to drive homewards, in the slanting rays of sunset, did the Towers of Chambord begin to look more attractive. The stunted aspect of the masonry became less perceptible, and with the last tint of rose-red light upon its lofty fleur-de-lys, Chambord, as we left it, seemed finer than it had been before. Châteaubriand's poetical description seemed more justified : the brilliant butterfly of the Renaissance striving to burst through its still visible chrysalis of Gothic traditions, the laced and ruffled head of the cavalier appearing above the strong joints of his armour, the beauty that was sought for and so nearly won, showed clearer than the failure which had at first oppressed us.

The drive back returns to Blois by a different

---

[1] Chiefly consisting in squares and diamonds of slate let into the surface of the stone.

road, and we came in sight of the cathedral with a
magnificent sunset sky behind it.   The darkening
river shone with a reflected golden light, while the
black towers above it stood out against a bank of
amber clouds that faded into violet and gray.

PART OF THE ROOF OF THE CHÂTEAU OF CHAMBORD, showing the lantern at the
top of the great staircase, and the decoration of the chimneys.

CHAPTER XXII

"Ce chasteau est ung des beaulx des gentils des mignons des mieulx élaborez chasteaulx de la mignonne Touraine, et se baigne tousiours en l'Indre comme une galloise princière."

THE Château of Azay-le-Rideau was built in 1520 by Gilles Berthelot, a relation of the Briçonnet, Beaune, and Bohier families, to whom Touraine owes so many of its graceful homes. It is remarkable not so much for its history[1] as for its extreme beauty as a type of the pure early French Renaissance architecture, untouched by the Italian influence of Primaticcio. The old fortress - dwelling is entirely discarded, nor is any attempt made, as at Chambord, to unite the feudal fortress to the hunting-seat. While Le Nepveu was actually attempting a "tour de force"

---

[1] The name is apparently derived from one Hugues Ridel, one of the knights-banneret of Touraine instituted by Philip Augustus, originally destined to command the road from Tours to Chinon. The old château was taken by the Burgundians in the reign of Charles VI., and retaken by the Dauphin in 1418, to be altogether rebuilt in the next century. Its new owner, Berthelot the financier, was involved in the usual distresses which seemed the inevitable portion of the Beaunes and Bohiers, and died of grief at Cambrai in 1529.

that from its very nature could but be doomed to
failure, the walls of Azay-le-Rideau were rising at
the bidding of a perfect and consistent plan. The
luxuriant fancy of the architect has given itself free
play in making as beautiful a dwelling-place as could
be well imagined, and using only those details of the
old fortress architecture which gave solidity to the
whole while they added to the picturesqueness of its
various parts. The old master masons had wellnigh
disappeared, and in their place had arisen the brilliant
school of Jean Bullant, of Pierre Lescot, of Jean
Goujon, who, while Maître le Roux and Le Primatice
were working at Fontainebleau, formed in France the
strong national artistic Renaissance that remained
almost untouched by innovations from the schools of
Rome and Florence.

Azay-le-Rideau is built in the form of an L upon
its side, with the entrance in the courtyard formed by
the meeting of the long arm of the letter with its
base. At each corner is placed with exquisite effect
a turreted and crested tower, and by an extremely
happy turn of the angle of the building which is
nearest to the entrance bridge across the river, an
effect of distance and beauty of line is secured unequalled among a series of architectural triumphs.

Nor is the setting of this rare building unworthy
of the gem it holds. Under the bridge, guarded by
two sculptured lions, flow the waters of the Indre,
that turn again in graceful curves beneath the

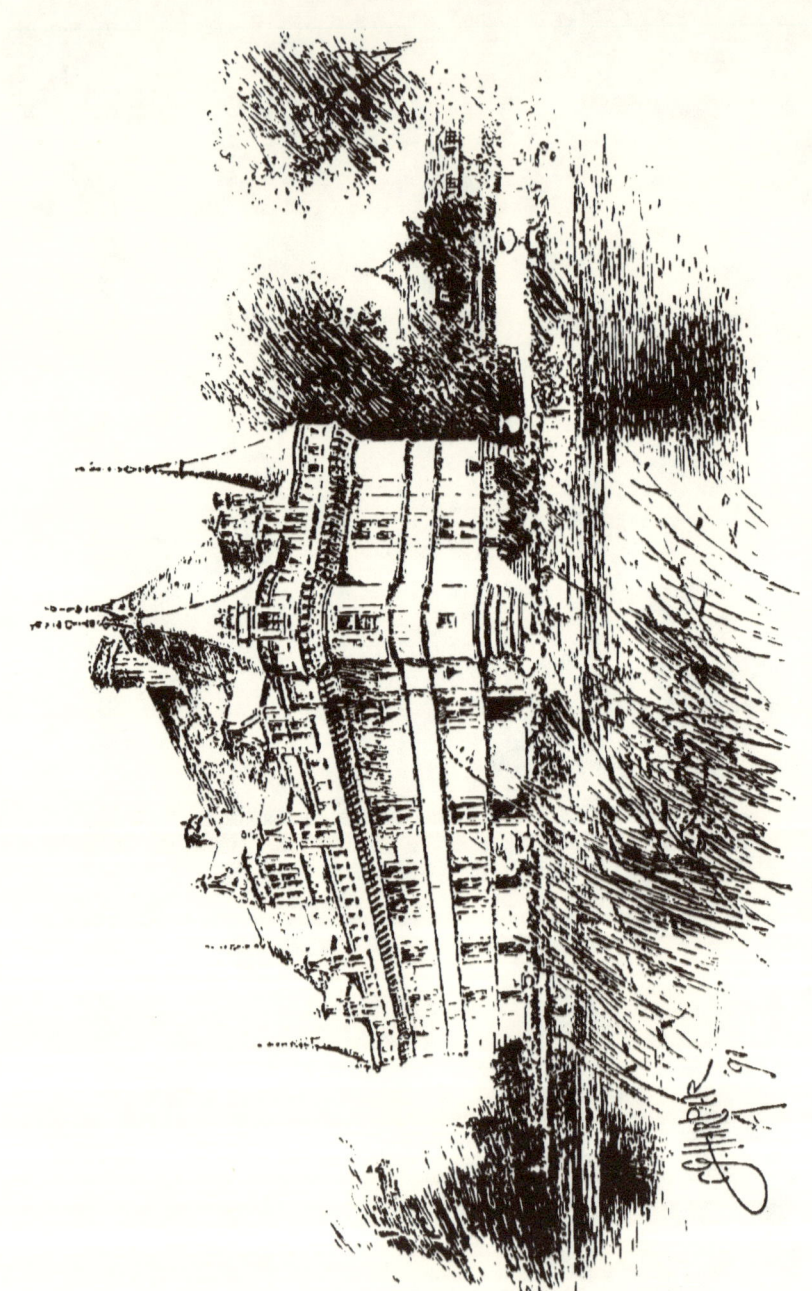

THE CHÂTEAU OF AZAY-LE-RIDEAU FROM ACROSS THE INDRE.

windows of the château, and are fringed with banks
of pleasant green shaded by limes and cedars. The
winding walks lead round towards the other side,
past a carved gallery of stone with curved steps
leading downwards from the windows to the water,
past the corner tower, to the long façade. Here, as
in the entrance court, the walls are covered with
carved panels, the bands that mark the different
stories are accentuated with graceful ornament, the very
chimney-tops are decorated with raised broidery, and
beneath the deep-cut line of the embrasures, marking
the low fall of the roof, the windows set in sculptured
frames have their full value and effect. Round the
next corner, in the quiet pool, swim the great carp
preserved for the table of the Marquis,[1] lazily floating
beneath the balcony that looks out upon the water.

Among the trees lies hidden a small chapel,
resonant with the rapid waters that fall in silver
foam upon each side and rush beneath its stone
floor ; and from this point a particularly charming
view of the angle that holds the central court within
may be obtained. It is in this central court that
the carving on the walls is brought to its greatest
perfection. Worthy in some parts of Jean Goujon's
chisel, it gives a singularly rich effect of fretted lace-
work among the lights and shadows of the graceful
corner towers, and, every pretence of fortification

---

[1] The present owner is M. le Marquis de Biencourt, by whom an
added grace of tasteful habitation is given to the rooms of Azay.

having been cast aside, rises to its highest excellence in the work above the entrance. Mrs. Mark Pattison gives the following description of it : " The first frieze shows bas-reliefs of the salamander of Francis I., and of the ermine of Claude of Brittany, his wife, who lay dying at Blois in July 1524, when this château was in course of building. On the plinth which supports the two windows of the pediment the same devices appear ; then a little arcade connects the ground floor with the upper stories, the pilasters and other members of which are covered with arabesques which may challenge comparison for beauty of design with the most exquisite passages produced at a later period."

Azay-le-Rideau should be seen last of the châteaux of Touraine, for as it is perhaps the most beautiful and perfect of them all, so its beauty gains by its association with all that is best and most attractive ; for in the shrine of Azay is gathered the whole gallery of faces of those who have made the history of Blois, of Amboise, of Chenonceaux, of France ; and the château, that is happy in its own lack of history and intrigue, gathers up within its sculptured walls the memories of all that was worth keeping of the old life that throbbed and struggled in the larger châteaux, and left them ruined or defaced. If the traveller who has seen the hot sunshine of the summer beat upon the walls of Loches and Chinon, or light up the halls of Blois, is so fortunate as to come to Azay in the cool, clear air of autumn, when the delicate colouring of its carven balconies is framed in the gold and crimson of the changing leaves, he will find, as we found, just such an ending to his own travels, just such a completion to his memories, as his imagination could desire.

No catalogue has yet been made of the most interesting pictures in this château ; but among them all should be picked out the exquisitely clear and careful presentment by F. Clouet of the face of Catherine de Medicis. This work is in the Chambre des Rois, where Francis I. and Louis XIV. slept on their various visits.[1]

Among many portraits of Francis I., perhaps that in the first guest-room is the best. There is the long nose, the insufferable smile upon his lips that curl upward satyr-like towards the narrow eyes, the crisp close-cut brownish beard, the pink silken sleeves and doublet. Above him, in stern contrast, hangs the face of Calvin.

But in the salon are the greatest treasures of the whole collection. Here is the charming Marie Stuart in youth, painted with exquisite care and refinement, with her young husband in the same frame beside her ; here is the great picture of Henry II. on horseback, with the interlacing letters on his harness that cover the walls of Chenonceaux ;[2] here are the haggard

---

[1] See list of pictures in the Appendix.
[2] See vol. i. p. 263.

eyes of Charles IX., full of the nameless terrors of
the wild night of St. Bartholomew, and weighed
down in mortal melancholy by the fatal counsels of
his mother.   Marguerite of Navarre is here as well,
and the relentless face of Anne de Montmorency,
the stern Constable, Coligny, white-haired and
venerable, and the weak revolting countenance of
Henry III.

Upon the other wall is the bright child's face of
Charles IX. before the plots of Catherine de Medicis
had wrecked him soul and body.   Near him is the
Pucelle d'Orléans and Philip of Burgundy ; while
Anne of Austria, still striving to be beautiful, is
showing off the " fairest hand and arm in France."

All the ages of French History look down upon
us from the panels as we pass.   In another guest-
room is the beautiful laughing face of Henrietta of
England, whose young husband with his effeminate
eyes and satin bows had watched us in the room
before.   Farther on is Mademoiselle de Montpensier
in the merry days of her girlhood, too cruelly placed
near the great red hat that shades her disappointed
face in later life.   Near to this is the small bourgeoise
head of the Pompadour, next her contemporary
Mademoiselle de l'Enclos, everlastingly invincible,
and opposite to these the stately figure of Madame
de Maintenon.

But the list grows long—of grave and gay, of
good and bad, all thrown together as they never were

in life, and all for the first time meeting under one
roof, never (let us hope) to be separated again.

"Old faces glimmered thro' the doors,
Old footsteps trod the upper floors."

There seemed a strange reality about this great
company of the illustrious dead. It must have been
here that Gautier dreamed of the old manor-house
where, as the evening falls, the portraits step down
from their frames.

"D'un reflet rouge illuminée
La bande se chauffe les doigts,
Et fait cercle à la cheminée
Où tout à coup flambe le bois.
L'image au sépulcre ravie
Perd son aspect roide et glacé,
La chaude pourpre de la vie
Remonte aux veines du passé."

It seemed no easy thing to step from so vivid
a resurrection of the past into the present that was
beneath, as we descended towards the entrance hall
by the fine staircase, the chief glory of the château,
that is panelled with the portraits of the kings of
France ; and where the towers of the old church [1]

[1] "There are some Angevine traces about the architecture of this
church," says Mr. Petit (*op. cit.*), "but the oldest part, now the north
aisle, the tower, and its eastern apse, seem, as in other instances, to have
constituted formerly the whole church."

Even in the eleventh century, when under the direction of the Abbey
of Corméry, this church is spoken of as old, and still shows traces of
ninth and tenth century work. There are some particularly curious
archaic statuettes and carvings along the front.

showed among the trees beyond the park, we wandered slowly back across the murmuring Indre, and
left Azay-le-Rideau veiled in the soft beauty of a
golden mist.

"Château du Souvenir, adieu!"

CHAPTER XXIII

THE TOWN OF TOURS AND ITS SURROUNDINGS

> "Monuments de la vieille France,
> Passé plus frais que l'avenir,
> Où trouverai-je une espérance
> Égale à votre souvenir ?"

WITH Chambord and Azay-le-Rideau the list is

CARDINAL DE RETZ

from the picture by (P. Van Schoopen).

ended of those typical castles in the valley of the Loire which must of necessity be visited. The history in which they bore a part ended in the story of the last Valois king at Blois. The school of architecture of which they furnish so many brilliant examples has reached its highest point of delicacy and perfection in the achievement of Azay. It only remains to indicate quite briefly a few of those castles which have been left almost unmentioned. Though of less interest, whether historical or architectural, than those already described, yet they cannot be omitted from the shortest sketch of what can be seen and learned in the extraordinary district between Blois and Saumur which, for want of a more accurate name, I have called " Old Touraine."

Blois, like Tours, is a centre from which it is possible to do much. Chambord and Chaumont we already know ; but there are two other châteaux, Cheverny and Beauregard, within a drive of Blois, which have yet to be explored. After keeping for a long time in the shadow of the forest, the road from Blois reaches the quiet little village of Cheverny, and a short distance farther on passes the old church of Cour-Cheverny with its fine roofed porch ; opposite to this is the gateway of the château, which is very large and white and modern - looking, built with pavilions on each side in the style of Versailles, and with the foundations with which Mansard had already familiarised us in the newest part of Blois.

The best pictures are in the grand salon, where is the face of the founder Philippe Hurault, Comte de Cheverny, Chancellor of France in the reign of Henry IV. Opposite to him is his wife Anne de Thou, a relation of the friend of the unhappy Cinq Mars, who perished on the same scaffold. Their daughter is above the mantelpiece, a Scotch-looking woman with black hair strung with pearls.

But the finest work of art in the whole château is the portrait of Cosmo de Medicis when quite young, which hangs on the right hand of the door ; it has unfortunately been retouched all round the face in 1827, but is not seriously damaged ; the treatment of the armour and lace, the masterly touches in the growth of the hair round the temples, and the magnificent breadth of the style would almost suggest that, did dates allow of it, this picture was the work of Titian.

In the next room is an excellent pencil sketch by Robert le Fevre of Charles X., with his falling under lip and high-bridged nose. The rest of the ground floor is chiefly decorated with the adventures of Don Quixote, painted on the panels of the gallery and dining-room.

A carved stone staircase leads to the Salle des Gardes above, which rejoices in an extremely well-preserved floor and ceiling, while the long row of tall windows looking out upon the park lights up to the full a room whose fine proportions are unconcealed by any attempt at furniture. The walls only, besides their appropriate decoration of trophies and suits of armour, are lined at the bottom with panel paintings of various flowers, each with a Latin motto. But the most extraordinary room in the château is the small " chambre des rois " beyond, wherein is the first parquetry made after tiles " went out." The walls are completely covered with tapestry and painting, and within this appropriate setting is the "legendary-looking bed" in which the good chancellor died in 1599.

On the left hand of the road that leads back to Blois, in the midst of the Forest of Russy, stands another château filled with pictures, with the appropriate name of Beauregard. There is the same strangely new appearance here as we had noticed at Cheverny, for probably little remains of the old château to which Jean du Thier (as Ronsard tells us) brought home in 1545 the Pindar and Simonides he had saved from Constantinople. The collection of pictures was begun by the minister Paul Ardier early in the seventeenth century, and composes a complete series of fifteen reigns down to Louis XIV., placed in the long gallery floored with tiles that represent a whole army of the reign of Louis XIV.; this must have been much as we see it now when Mademoiselle de Montpensier came to visit De Vineuil here and talked over the intrigues of the Fronde and the doings of the great Condé.

Besides these pictures—there are some three hundred and fifty of them—there is not much to see save a charming sketch by Watteau in the drawing-room, of the Duchesse de Dino, the châtelaine at the beginning of the present century.

Before travelling westward again, there is Ramorantin to be seen, where Louise de Savoie first brought up her young son Francis, and where later on she saw the comet in the sky that presaged his success at Marignano. Upon the banks of the Cher is Montrichard, one of the many strongholds of Foulques Nerra, and now terribly damaged by the vandalism of 1793 ; on almost every eminence that rises from the vine-clad plains the traveller

> " Découvre du vieux manoir
> Les tourelles en poivrière
> Et les hauts toits en éteignoir,"

and nearly all are filled with memories of the Fronde ; for here the chief actors in those troublous times came to repose a little from the feverish intrigues of Paris, to talk a little quiet scandal, like De Retz, or to lie "perdue" till the storm blew over, like Madame de Chevreuse and many more of the "beautés de qualité," who mixed up politics with gallantry and claimed the lead in both.

From his château east of Loches, between the Indre and the Cher, the Duc de Montrésor would ride across to Tours to talk to Madame de Chevreuse of the impossibility of rousing Gaston d'Orléans to anything approaching consistent policy or courageous support to his allies ; or stop at Montbazon, a little farther northward down the Indre, to hear the latest news of Marie de Rohan's quarrel with the Duchesse de Longueville. Of Montbazon little is left now save " the ruins of a castle, built when men knew how to build, upon a rock with turrets lichen-gilded

like a rock," and even in those times it seems to
have fallen into disrepair, for the family lived chiefly
at the Château of Couzières, where the tale still
lingers of the terrible end that befell the Duchesse
de Montbazon, whose beauty De Retz praises so
highly and whose vices even he cannot condone. In
a famous sentence he has summed her up : " Je n'ai
jamais vu personne qui eût conservé dans le vice si
peu de respect pour la vertu."

The last of her lovers was one Armand de Rancé,
an ecclesiastic of easy morals, like the Coadjutor
himself, who " preached like an angel all the forenoon,
and hunted like a devil all the evening." The beauty
of Marie de Rohan, perhaps too the strange attraction
of her wild and unrestrained abandonment in the
pursuit of pleasure, on horseback or afoot, had completely fascinated the Abbé de Rancé ; with one last
effort to shake off the spell he accepted the chance of
employment in negotiations with the Vatican. But
he could not stay in Italy ; in the groves of the
Campagna, in the corridors of the Vatican, the
memory of Marie was with him still, and he could
not rest away from her. After a hurried journey
back he rode to the Château of Couzières late on an
evening, too wrapped up in his own thoughts to see
a strange air of sudden desolation in the place, or
notice that the servants were in black ; he was on
familiar ground, and was soon through the side-door
and mounting the secret staircase to her room.

There were two candles burning in it as he entered, with a faint light that showed him the duchess lying on her bed ; he rushed across the room and kissed her passionately upon the lips ; the white face fell from him heavily, and her head rolled down between his feet.

How the unhappy lover fled from the room, with what thoughts of a husband's vengeance, of the terrible greeting that had been placed for him, we know not ; but it was Armand de Rancé who was the first Abbé Commandataire de la Trappe, and sought perhaps, in the silence of the Trappiste monasteries, forgetfulness.[1]

It was to Couzières that Marie de Medicis came from Montbazon, after she had escaped from the Château of Blois and had been persuaded to leave Angoulême ; De Retz and Luynes had met her at Poitiers, and at Couzières the Dukes of Guise and Montbazon joined them, to witness her reconciliation with Louis XIII., after which the whole Court left, with an exaggerated gaiety, to see the fêtes at Tours.

The château from which the Maréchal de Luynes, the King's favourite, took his title is close to Tours,

[1] Such is the legend : the truth (as far as it will ever be known) is almost as strange. While De Rancé was away a sudden attack of smallpox had killed the Duchess, who was one of the finest riders and tallest women of her time ; the coffin that was hurriedly provided for her burial had proved too short, and the corpse could only be put in without its head, which was cut off and laid upon a silver tray ; and this was what the Abbé saw.

a little westward down the Loire; it stands upon a
hill looking down upon the fields that slope toward
the river, and is approached by a fine bridge very
like that at Chinon.   The place was called Maillé[1]
before Louis XIII. had given his favourite the title,
and there are still standing relics of a far older time,
in the great Roman aqueduct which bore the waters
of the stream behind the Church of St. Vernant to
the fort which defended the old road to Le Mans.[2]

The name of yet another favourite in the same
reign is recalled by the strange Pile de Cinq Mars, a
little farther down the valley.   An explanation has
already been suggested for this strange erection; it
may well have flashed signals for the Lanterne de
Rochecorbon to pass on to Amboise, but no reason-
able account of its building and design has been as
yet forthcoming.   Upon the hill a little higher up are
the ruins of a château, three round towers, the smallest
with a pointed roof, and lower down a smaller tower,
detached, that may have been the outworks of the
entrance gate.   It is appropriate that the memorials
of so sad a fate, of so unexplained a character, should
be ruins as strange and as decayed as these; De
Vigny has told the whole sad story of the sudden
rise to power, the hopeless love, the whole career of
Cinq Mars, from his leaving home at Chaumont till

[1] *Malliacense Castrum* (Mabille).
[2] These ruins were ruins already in the time of Gregory of Tours,
who says of the convent there, "ab antiquis vallatum aedificiis jam
erutis."

TOMB OF ARMAND DU PLESSIS RICHELIEU (carved by Girardon).

his execution with De Thou. It is but one more trace of the sinister influence of Richelieu, who built one of the towns in Touraine, with whose memory all these Castles of the Fronde are filled. It was down the Loire that the Cardinal was borne in his last illness, in the vast litter which was carried into the towns at night, where gates built only for an ordinary prince were far too narrow, through breaches battered in the walls, as though by a besieging army. Many breathed more freely in the town of Richelieu,[1] and in all Touraine, when that strong spirit passed away. "Il avait assez de religion pour ce monde," says the broad-minded De Retz, "il anéantissait par son pouvoir et par son faste royal la majesté personnelle du roi," and it was for this mastery over the King, for this subjection in which he held all France, that Richelieu was chiefly hated in Touraine, one of the last strongholds of the feudal nobility who had opposed him to the last.

We have drawn very close now to our journey's end, to the town of Tours itself. Upon the other side, eastwards, is the tall shaft poised upon a precipice which is known as the Lanterne de Rochecorbon; it is all that is left of the "chastel deschiqueté et taillade comme ung pourpoinct hespaignol," which Messire Bruyn built when he returned from the crusades to marry his young wife.

The next estates to his were those of the great

---

[1] A few miles south of Chinon.

Abbey of Marmoutier,[1] within which the seven sleepers slept for five-and-twenty years, and apparently re-mained in unchanged slumber after death. The little cells within the solid rock wherein St. Martin and St. Gatien lived and prayed, are still to be seen ; but the modern buildings (of the Sacred Heart) con-trast somewhat too sharply with the bygone religious memories which the place unconsciously awakens, and which are preserved in the old door and short-ened spire, alone, that face the entrance. But the impressions of the modern Marmoutier are at least far preferable to the terrible disappointment that awaits the visitor to Plessis-lez-Tours ; he must boldly discard the vision that the scenes of *Quentin Dur-ward* conjured up, he must approach with more than one sense blunted to the possibilities of offence, for the abode of the once " dreadful Louis " is reduced to an evil-smelling shed filled with the carts of the night scavengers.

There can still be traced (chiefly in the imagina-tion of the attendant ghoul) the outline and the walls and ditches of the park, the little nook beneath a stairway where Balue was hidden in his cage, and certain problematical and earthy hollows which are supposed to lead by subterranean passages to the town of Tours ; at their other end was the house of Tristan l'Hermite ; the house that is called his, at any rate exists, and though nearly certainly built in

[1] This word is said to be " *maius monasterium.*"

the next century, it is worth a visit for its own sake ;
for the outside, which is decorated with a twisted
cord (at once put down as the somewhat too obvious
badge of Tristan's office), has a quiet harmony of
colour in the lines of brick and stone ; and the little
court within, from which rises a tall tower with a
winding stair, is a pretty example of the domestic
architecture of the time.

The presence of the Court at Plessis, which was
not always so offensive after all, was often the occasion of festivities in the Town.   Mystery Plays, pro-
cessions, and receptions often occupied the good
citizens, who, as we have seen, were quite capable of
taking their part in anything artistic.   Their trade,
too, flourished ; in the birthplace of Jean Fouquet, of
Michel Colombe, of François Clouet, the arts were
not likely to fall into neglect, and in 1546 the
Venetian Marino de' Cavalli notices one branch of
industry in which those arts were used, " the manu-
factories of silken work and tapestry at Tours," he
says, " are of the best in France ; " the silk from Spain
and Italy was sent there, and Venetian workmen
were encouraged to come over to teach the Tour-
angeaux all that they knew of weaving broidery and
tissues.   In the year before this, just as the right-
hand tower of the Cathedral was being brought to its
completion, a Royal Charter had been granted for two
fairs at Tours in March and in September, at which
" silks and cloth of gold and silver, as good and fine

as those of any foreign manufacture," were always
on sale. These great fairs stopped in 1616, but were
revived again in 1782, and still take place each winter
and summer along the Quai beside the Loire.

One of the great features of the public reception
given to Charles IX.[1] was an arch with an inscription
referring to

> " La Soye, honneur de cette ville,
> Donnant la vie aux peuples avec leurs mains."

Immediately after the Colonel of Infantry, in the
procession that came out to greet the King, was the
Company of Silk-makers clad in black velvet hats
with green cord, in leather of the King's colour, pourpoints of " taffetas cramoisy " and black collars.
Mercers, armourers, and jewellers followed, and a
brave array of butchers " who were magnificently
dressed and very brawny men," wearing blue hats
and scarlet doublets. Last came the " Sieurs de la
Bazoche," the town company of actors, " who had
right cunningly secured permission from the Silk
Mercers, par une invention rare et magnifique," to
wear " taffetas cramoisy," and black velvet hats as
well.

The next royal reception was to Henry III. and
his mother, in which devices were scattered throughout the town with complimentary references to the

---

[1] See *La description de l'entrée du très Chrétien Roy Charles IX. du
nom, en sa ville de Tours*, par Jehan Cloppel, à Tours par Ollivier
Tafforeau Imprimeur demeurant près les Cordeliers, 1565, a rare little
book in the Bibliothèque Nationale.

peace-loving virtues and general amiability of Catherine de Medicis. Tours was at this time in great happiness and prosperity, and Girolamo Lippomano, the Venetian, sends home a glowing account of the pastures and beeves, the wine, the fruit, the corn, that grew in such abundance, the silks and merchandise that vied with goods from Naples and from Lucca.

But the town was not to be wholly untouched by the political and religious quarrels of the sixteenth century. In 1588, certain printers found themselves forced to quit Paris after the disturbances at the end of Henry III.'s reign, and fled to Tours, where they formed a society for the publication of certain works in demand.[1] Their deed and agreement is still in existence.

The beginning of 1589 was an agitated time in many ways for the town that was so near the place where Guise had been murdered ; a more interesting

[1] See "Une Association d'imprimeurs et de libraires de Paris réfugiés à Tours au xvi. siècle. Janet Mettayer. Marc Orry. Claude de Montr'œil. Jehan Richer. Matthieu Guillemot. Sébastien du Molin. Georges de Robet. Abel Langellier." Tours, imp. Rouillé Ladevèze, 1878, 8vo. Their publications are rather rare, and I have only seen two, which are *Recueil de la Harangue faicte à l'ouverture du Parlement*, par M. C. Servain, 1589, and *La Pucelle d'Orléans Restituée*, par Jean Beroalde de Verulle, 1599.

The first Guide-book I can discover for the town and district was published in 1592 by Isaac François Sieur de la Girardie at Tours.

L. Vitet in *La Ligue* gives a list of the many political pamphlets published at this time, in a small duodecimo edition, with narrow margins, and thick type such as the *Machiavel*, printed at Tours, which Henry III. was reading just before the murder of the Duc de Guise.

meeting than any seen that century came off in the
gardens of Plessis when Henry of Navarre came from
the Protestant assembly at La Rochelle, the only one
of all his suite who had a cloak to wear or a feather
in his hat, the famous "panache blanche" that led
the way at Ivry.

The last of the Valois embracing the first of the
Bourbons must have been a strange sight for those
of the courtiers who had watched the long struggle
between the three Henrys ; but now Guise was dead,
and Catherine de Medicis, his bitterest enemy, was
gone, there was nothing to hinder the King of Navarre from coming forward to take his true position.
The murder of the King by Jacques Clément still
further cleared his pathway to the throne of France,
and with his reign the next century seemed at last
likely to have rest from civil wars.

Tours itself had not escaped the last efforts of
the League—there had been hard fighting on the
bridge and in the faubourg of St. Symphorien, from
which Mayenne's men were only with difficulty dis-
lodged, after several churches had suffered terribly
from the rude treatment of the defenders of the
Catholic Faith.

One more reminder of De Guise's murder remained
in a tower of the Fortress by the river—his young
son, the Prince de Joinville, had been imprisoned
there, and in 1593 escaped with singular daring
and success.   On his way to mass, he suddenly laid

HENRY IV., KING OF FRANCE.

a wager with his guards that he could run upstairs again quicker than they could ; he reached his room first, bolted the door, and with a long cord which had been brought him by his laundress, slipped out of window with a bar between his legs, and dropped from fifteen feet. With shots whistling round his ears, he rushed round the walls to the Faubourg de la Riche, where he found a baker's horse and leaped upon its back ; the saddle turned round and threw him, and a soldier came up suddenly—it was no enemy, but by a happy chance, a Leaguer who gave him a fresh mount ; in a few moments he was past the town and had soon put the Cher between himself and his pursuers.

The town still prospered ; and its manufactures had received further encouragement by the Edict of Nantes about 1598. The King had even ordered mulberry trees to be planted round Paris, Tours, and Orleans, and the first book published on the art of silk-making appeared, by one Jean Baptiste Letellier. But the next century saw a terrible change.

The question of religion now becomes inextricably mixed up with the commercial issues which are at stake, for at the head of the silk-weaving industry were the numerous families of Huguenots who for some time had been flourishing within the town ; nor had their presence there been without suffering ; so far back as 1544, persecutions had begun in the

town [1] of those heretics whose doctrines were first
heard of twenty years before. Some of the leading
Huguenots were even taken to Paris to be burnt, to
serve as a more striking warning to the rest. At
last in 1562 came the inevitable result of the
massacre at Amboise. In the library at Tours is
a horribly faithful representation of the slaying of
the Huguenots throughout the town, and even in
boats and barges on the river. There was of course
vengeance upon the other side, when Condé's army
ten years later opened the town again to the
victorious Protestants, and towards the end of the
century the presence of Henry of Navarre did much
to strengthen the Huguenot cause. At last it seemed
possible, in spite of sudden outbursts of fanaticism,
that the two religions should live side by side. The
Huguenots, moreover, had justified their presence by
their skill in arts and industries, particularly in the
silk manufacture, which was always the staple of
commerce of the place.

Suddenly, upon 16th May 1685, the Revocation
of the Edict of Nantes fell like a thunderclap upon
the town. The Huguenots dispersed to Switzerland, to Holland, to the southern shores of England,
even to America, carrying the secrets of their commerce with them, and, what was worse, followed by
their workmen. Out of a total of eighty thousand

---

[1] See the excellent little work on *Protestantism in Touraine* by M.
Dupin St. André, now Minister at Tours.

inhabitants, fifty thousand went ; the silk industry was destroyed or carried across the Channel, to enrich the English at the expense of whole populations of the working French.

It is not too much to say that the town never recovered from the shock ; it is only in the last ten years that the old prosperity seems coming back again.[1] Already much of what John Evelyn saw, when he came here for nineteen weeks, " took a master of the language and studied very diligently," is gone for ever. " Both the church and monastery of Martin are large," he writes, speaking of buildings which now exist only in name,[2] " having four square towers, fair organs, and a stately altar, where they show the bones and ashes of St. Martin, with other reliques. The Mall without comparison is the noblest in Europe for length and shade, having seven rows of the tallest and goodliest elms I had ever beheld, the innermost of which do so embrace each other and at such a height that nothing can be more solemn or majestical. . . . No city in France exceeds it in beauty or delight." This was written before the Revocation had devastated the

---

[1] The years after the Revocation of the Edict were unprosperous for many reasons besides the loss of the silk industry : it was the time when the inequality and injustice of taxation so convincingly pointed out by De Tocqueville was at its height. Even in 1761 the *Société d'Agriculture* at Tours writes to complain bitterly of the unfair pressure of certain feudal rights on the country populations.

[2] Save for the two towers, with a waste of street between, melancholy landmarks of the great church that once existed.

town.   Evelyn saw, too, the tomb of Ronsard, who
died at St. Cosmo in 1585, in the chapel of Plessis-
lez - Tours, and was so fortunate as to meet the
Queen of England, who was entertained at the archbishop's palace on her way to Paris.

Great efforts had been made to restore the sink-
ing fortunes of the town, and when Arthur Young
came here in 1787, he could speak of the " new
street (the Rue Royale) of large houses, built of
hewn white stone with regular fronts," which had
just been laid out, though even now several of the
owners refuse to incur the expense of filling up the
design.   " They ought, however, to be unroosted if
they will not comply," cries the Englishman.   He
saw too several fine pictures in the chapel at Plessis,
and heard with regret that the corporation had
offered the old trees in the Park for sale.   " One
would not wonder," he reflects frankly enough, " at
an English corporation sacrificing the ladies' walk
for plenty of turtle, venison, and madeira ; but that
a French one should have so little gallantry is
inexcusable."

But worse things than this were soon to happen.
In 1792 the town was celebrating a fête to Liberty,
and all the châteaux in the valley suffered in the
general turmoil.   The citizens were busy listening
to the " Hymn to Great Men," to a " Discourse to
the Nations," to a " Hymn to Reason," or singing
tumultuously after this fashion—

" Les ennemis du nom français
Sur Tours ont formé des projets,
Mais on les attend là,
À Tours on les fera
Voir de vrais sansculottes ;
Vive le son
Du canon !"

In 1815 the enemy were at the gates in earnest : the Prussians and the Allies were encamped in St. Symphorien.

But after the fever of the Revolution had somewhat calmed, after the terrible fighting in La Vendée had ceased, Tours began slowly and steadily to recover, in a quiet prosperous time of harvest and repose. These were the days when English most did congregate at Tours. The handbook of 1841 reports two English churches, where not one now exists, and speaks of the trout fishing to be had, and of the seventy English families who throve and multiplied in their new colony among the vineyards.

The war of 1870 seems to have frightened them away. In the autumn of that year Léon Gambetta, escaping in his balloon from Paris, carried on the Government in the Palais de Justice of Tours before the Assembly at Bordeaux was constituted. It was in that winter that the Germans occupied the heights above the town, which was absolutely incapable of making any defence. But the traces of the so-called " siege " have vanished, and the town has resumed its quiet advance towards material prosperity.

The statue of Balzac looks down the Rue
Royale he loved so well, towards the Quai where
Rabelais and Descartes look upon the town ; behind them stretches the valley of the Loire.   It is
a fascinating valley, full of history, full of romance.
The Plantagenets have lived and died here, the
Black Prince has fought up and down the river, Sir
Walter Raleigh served his first campaign here with
the Protestants, even King Arthur has been heard
of at Amboise.   Here are scenes that Turner has
painted, where Landor and Wordsworth have watched
the setting sun ; here in the heart of France, in
the most French of all her provinces, there seems a
special interest for the Englishman, a special beauty
in this royal river flowing past Fontevrault to the sea,
in this broad smiling landscape clad with vines,

> "Where from the frequent bridge,
>   Like emblems of infinity,
>   The trenched waters run from sky to sky."

APPENDIX

THE traveller may find it convenient to have a few other places in Tours and its neighbourhood pointed out for his especial notice. Information concerning them is easily procurable (especially from the books already recommended), and they are collected here merely to avoid his missing them. Between the two best hotels, the Hôtel de l'Univers and the Hôtel du Faisan, there is very little choice; the first is on the Boulevards not far from the main line station, the second in the Rue Royale : both are good. The Rue Royale (or Nationale, according to your politics) runs straight through the town from the Palais de Justice on the Boulevards to the great stone bridge over the Loire. At No. 39 Balzac was born. On the Quai to the right, in what is now a barrack, is the Tour de Guise. In visiting the Cathedral, the traveller should especially notice the old glass in the choir, the tomb of Charles VIII.'s children, and the extraordinary staircase poised upon the keystone of an arch, by which he will be conducted to the summit of one of the towers. Two great towers are all that is left of St. Martin's Cathedral and Abbey. Near the Tour de Charlemagne the Cloister of St. Martin must particularly be seen, as one of the finest examples of Renaissance carving in the town. The date of this cloister is given as 1508 in p. 141 of M. Grandmaison's *Documents Inédits pour Servir à l'Histoire des Arts en Touraine.* The Church of St. Julien, too, near the Rue Royale, should be visited : it had been begun by the historian Gregory of Tours in 576, was destroyed in 856 by the Normans, and of the later church little but the western tower of eleventh-century work remains ; the present structure is chiefly of the fourteenth century, and has not long been restored to its present state from the terrible decay and disrepair into which it had fallen. In 1817, Mr. W. D. Fellowes, who has published notes of his travels on the way to the Monastery of La Trappe, arrived at Tours and notices its foot pavement in the Rue Royale, "a thing seldom to be met with in this country," though at that time Tours was almost an English colony. The traveller was put up in the " Hôtel St. Julien." In the side aisles of the church were stalls for horses and cattle, the centre was a "remise " for carriages.

The Bank in the Rue de Commerce, where circular notes are exchanged, is the famous Hôtel Gouin, a beautiful example of early French Renaissance. The Hôtel de Beaune, in the Rue St. François, is another example of the same type, and the chimneypiece in the Hôtel de la Boule d'Or must also be seen. The house of Tristan l'Hermite has been already mentioned. In the Place du Grand Marché is a fine fountain put up in 1510 by Jacques de Beaune Semblançay, whose house is in the corner of the same square. M. Grandmaison publishes the details of the fountain's construction from the archives of Tours. Its four blocks of marble came from Genoa. Michel Colombe directed the sculptors, Bastien and Martin les François. It was originally surmounted by a crown and flowers, above which was a bronzed and gilt crucifixion, but all these ornaments have now disappeared. There is an excellent theatre in the Rue de la Scelleric, nearly opposite the best bookseller. Baths in the Loire are to be found on the island which helps to support the suspension bridge ; and there is a good library.

At St. Symphorien across the river is a quaint Roman-esque cross church, "swamped by a flamboyant nave," with a good western door. At St. Radegonde, farther to the east along the bank, the church is built against the rock, in which a chapel is excavated that communicates with the tower. The Abbey of Marmoutier is in the same direction. Crossing the river again, on the far side of the town to the south and west the traveller will find Plessis-lez-Tours and the Abbey of St. Como. Still farther out into the country is the Romanesque church of Villandry, which, says Mr. Petit, "combines in itself the chief characteristics one or other of which is found in most churches of this district." The château there, too, with the beautiful flower-beds sur-rounding it, is well worth a visit. The finest conservatories in Touraine, almost in France, are to be seen at M. Mame's château of Les Touches, near Savonnières, not far from Ballan ; there are also some strange grottos, "caves gout-tières," in the neighbourhood. Mr. Fellowes in 1817 seems to have made a strangely fragmentary visit. Out of all the châteaux he chose only Chanteloup, Ménard, the favourite home of Madame de Pompadour, and Valançay, the seat of M. de Talleyrand, from which the English Government failed in its attempt to rescue Ferdinand VII. of Spain by means of a certain mysterious foreign baron.

One more excursion may be advised, to the Château d'Ussé, now in the possession of the Comte de Blacas, the heir of Madame la Comtesse de la Rochejaquelein, an

exceedingly picturesque old pile in well-kept grounds near
the junction of the Indre with the Loire. There are some
interesting rooms and some good pictures, especially in the
Gallerie de Vauban. The greatest treasure there is what is
known as the "Buste d'Ussé," a Florentine work of the late
fifteenth century; it formerly was in the collection of the
famous Fouquet, and M. Léon Palustre considers that it
represents Hercule, Duc de Ferrara (1471-1505). In any
case, it is one of the finest pieces of portrait sculpture to be
seen in Touraine, not excepting the bust of Francis near
Loches, and it should on no account be missed. Many
places might yet be mentioned, but the typical châteaux
and churches have been pointed out, and in the map,
which shows only a few details for the sake of being quite
clear, their relative position and accessibility can be quickly
seen. Further information can be easily procured, and as
to railways the useful *Guide Bijou d'Indre et Loire* may be
safely and profitably used. The inns are almost uniformly
good and clean.

II.—MANUSCRIPTS AND BOOKS

The town is particularly fortunate in the abundance of
Manuscripts and Documents which it possesses. In the
Archives Départmentales d'Indre et Loire, kept in the
Prefecture, are great quantities of title-deeds and records
preserved from the old religious houses, among which is the
grant of Louis le Débonnaire in 837 to found the Abbey
of Corméry, with a seal attached, a deed of Hugh Capet,
and other treasures; in the Hôtel de Ville are the Archives
Communales, which are among the most important in
France. Mgr. Chevalier gives a list of their contents.
Detailed accounts of parish expenses since 1358 are

preserved, municipal documents since 1408, and numbers of letters and other manuscripts from 1140 onwards. The political archives stretch fairly continuously from the English occupation in 1347 to 1815 and Waterloo. Many most valuable facts with reference to the old Mystery Plays and theatrical representations are also to be found here (copied by M. André Salmon), and the diligence of M. Grandmaison has brought to light all that is known of the Clouets, and especially of Jean Clouet II., whose illuminated Livy is preserved in the town library, which also contains the *Hours* of Charles V. and of Anne of Brittany, a thirteenth-century Terence, and many other rarities. But the librarian shall describe them himself. "La Bibliothèque de Tours, installée rue Nationale 90, dans les bâtiments de l'ancienne fabrique royale de soieries (lampas et damas de Tours), contient aujourd'hui cent mille volumes environ. Ils proviennent, en grande partie, des librairies ou bibliothèques des abbayes et couvents qui existaient autrefois à Tours. Notons particulièrement les riches et précieux fonds des Bénédictins de l'abbaye de Marmoutier, des chanoines de la collégiale de Saint Martin, et de l'église métropolitaine de Saint Gatien. Dans la série de Manuscrits, au nombre de près de 1800, on remarque plusieurs *Sacramentaires*, sortis de l'École d'enluminure et de calligraphie à Tours, fondée par le célèbre Alcuin au VIIIme siècle. L'un d'eux, écrit en lettres d'or sur magnifique vélin et remontant au VIIIme siècle, est l'évangéliaire sur lequel les rois de France prêtaient serment lorsqu'ils étaient reçus abbés honoraires de Saint Martin." This MS. was collated in 1884 with that in the British Museum ; it is one of the finest specimens of its kind in the world, and in almost perfect preservation. A MS. of Ovid has also been published by the Clarendon Press in

1888, and a Hebrew Bible of the fifteenth century was annotated in 1884.

" Dans les documents liturgiques d'un grand intérêt," continues M. Duboz, " on remarque un Missel à l'usage de l'église anglicane (*sic*) ; ce manuscrit, qui a appartenu primitivement à la famille de Hungerford, devint la propriété des seigneurs de Bueil. Notons encore un ravissant manuscrit persan contenant les poésies de Hafiz, intitulées "Le Divan." Enfin d'importants documents sur l'histoire de la Touraine, copiés dans divers dépôts publics de l'Angleterre, sont aujourd'hui conservés dans cette bibliothèque, qui n'est pas moins riche en éditions du commencement de l'imprimerie ; elle possède plus de 400 *Incunables*, parmi lesquels se trouvent un superbe exemplaire de la Bible de Mayence (1462), un exemplaire unique des 'Coutumes de Touraine,' et un magnifique Missel sur vélin à l'usage de Tours (1485)." The library is open every week-day (except fête-days) from 1st April to 30th September from 12 till 6 ; from 1st October till 30th March from 10 A.M. till 4, and from 7 P.M. till 9.30.

III.—PICTURES

The valley of the Loire is peculiarly rich in pictures by Jean and François Clouet and their school. At Chenonceaux, among many other valuable portraits, is a fine Catherine de Medicis and a clean-shaven monkish-looking head of Henry III. At Azay-le-Rideau is the richest collection of all—another Henry III., dressed very much like a woman, an excellent half-length of Charles IX., and many other examples of the Clouets, of De Brissac, and Corneille de Lyon ; best of all is the equestrian portrait which is reproduced in Chapter XII. of this book. Mrs. Mark

Pattison has described it as follows. "The King is represented about half life-size on horseback. He wears a rich Court costume of black relieved by white, and the trappings of his horse show the same colours. . . . The sombre figure of the mounted King, swarthy, difficult of speech, gazing outwards with concentrated intention, habited in black, and set in a framework of gray half tones, haunts the recollection with the vividness of actual vision; for the subject, which seems to offer in itself weird suggestions of a phantom magic, is realised with tangible definiteness of conception, and rendered with unflinching fidelity to the solid aspect of real life." Other fine pictures in the collection of the Marquis de Biencourt at Azay-le-Rideau are the portrait of Ambroise Paré, surgeon of Henry III., in the library, and of Monsieur, brother of Louis XIV., in the same room. At my last visit to Azay-le-Rideau, almost a year after Chapter XXII. was written, there were a few changes in the arrangement of the pictures, which will be noticed in comparing my description of them with what a visitor may be shown at present. Clouet's "Catherine de Medicis" (for instance) is now removed to the upper rooms. A few more pictures in this same treasure-house of art should also be noticed. Next to the Clouet of Charles IX. is another by the same artist and with the same green background, of Odet de Coligny. Other examples of F. Clouet are the "Claude, wife of Francis I." and the "Henry VIII. of England"; pictures of this school are "La Reine Margot" and "Marguerite de Navarre." There are also some exceptionally fine bronze medallions in the lower passage, representing Catherine de Medicis, Henry II., Charles IX., and Henry III. In the private room of M. le Marquis de Biencourt are Marie de Medicis, perhaps by Rubens, the Maréchal de Luxembourg, and Turenne by Champagne,

whose finest example here is the Marie de Medicis on
the lower floor. The portraits of Marie Leczinska (in red),
and her husband are also good, and there are several
copies of Cardinal Fleury with the same placid smile, and
soft white cloak excellently rendered; with many more
which well deserve a closer inspection than will be possible
for most travellers.

The pictures at the Château of Cheverny must also be
seen. The immense gallery of historical portraits at Beauregard are remarkable more for their interest and variety
than for any especial artistic merit : they leave the impression of having all been done by the same hand. The
series begins upon the wall in which the entrance door
opens, and at the spectator's right hand of that wall, begin-
ing at Philippe de Valois, born in 1328, and going from
right to left entirely round the room. They are roughly
divided into reigns by divisions in the panels. In the
second division are Philippe de Commines, Cæsar Borgia,
and a good portrait of Anne de Bretagne looking fat and
comfortable, but determined; in the third division are the
Cardinal d'Amboise (very different from the more spirited
likeness at Chaumont) and Amerigo Vespucci; in the
fourth, Florimond Robertet is the best. There is also a
portrait of Sir Thomas More. In the fifth are " François
Pisarre " and Diane de Poitiers ; in the sixth, Jehan
Destre, " Grand Maistre d'Artillerie " with a beard like a
puff of smoke; in the seventh, Marie Stuart in a high
collar ; in the eighth, Henri de Guise and Francis Drake ;
in the ninth, Elizabeth, Queen of England, in old age, and
what is perhaps the best piece of work in the room, a large
Henry IV. on horseback, with his good-natured face and
gray beard beneath a most strange helmet, surrounded by
D'Arnaud, Biron, and Sully. The tenth and last division

has a portrait of the famous "Duc de Bukinkan," a very feeble production after the handsome face of Villiers at Hampton Court. In the museums at Blois and at Tours there are also a very few good pictures which must be picked out from a mass of inferior painting.

Of the historical portraits in the École Française at the Louvre Galleries in Paris only two can be ascribed with certainty to François Clouet. Among all the examples of the École Clouet, the two finest are those numbered 107 and 108 in the catalogue edited by M. Frédéric Villot. The first is that of Charles IX., a small full-length figure, three-quarter face, with black coat buttoned to the ruff and embroidered with gold ; the right hand, carrying his gloves, rests on the back of a red velvet sofa ; two green curtains form the background : a copy of this, life-size, exists in the Imperial Gallery at Vienna. The second is the portrait of his wife, Elizabeth of Austria ; her head is turned to the left, three-quarter face, the hair lifted up from the forehead : she wears a rich gold necklace, and a dress of cloth of gold embroidered with precious stones. These two portraits may be taken as types of François Clouet's style, in distinguishing copies from the few productions that are left of this master's actual handiwork. No. 109, a head of Francis I., of extreme delicacy and accuracy of presentment, is also probably by a Clouet, but whether by Jean or by his son François cannot be determined ; it looks as if the basis of the painting were a thin gold or silver background on which the surface tints were afterwards applied. In the same room is another portrait of Francis I., two of Henry II., one full length, the other of smaller size, perhaps a copy, wearing the medallion of the Order of St. Michael and the same black dress striped with gold. No. 113 is François de Lorraine, Duc de Guise ; No. 124 is Catherine de

Medicis. Note also No. 732, Gaspard de Coligny; 729, Charles IX.; and 653, "le très victorieux Roy de France, Charles VII.," a repulsive face beneath a hideous hat. No. 656 (a ball at the Court of Henry III.) will give a good idea of the costume of the latter half of the sixteenth century. These last are all by unknown artists.

It may help to complete this note if I mention very briefly a few places in England where pictures by the Clouets and their school exist, or where the portraits of persons connected with Touraine may be seen. First and foremost is the great collection at Hampton Court, which contains Eleanor of Spain, wife of Francis I., by Jean Clouet (No. 561 in the Catalogue published by Mr. Ernest Law), and a Francis I. attributed to Holbein, which Mrs. Mark Pattison considers to be by a French hand (No. 598 in the same Catalogue). This portrait gives an extraordinary sense of nakedness; the complexion is of an almost porcine pink, and the expression brutal. There is also a portrait of a boy, attributed to Janet, described as the Dauphin François, son of Henry II. The writer already quoted considers this to be Henry III. in youth, and says, "Perhaps the whole of François Clouet's work does not afford a better example than the Hampton Court portrait, of that art of giving life which was attributed to him in chief by his contemporaries." In the same collection note No. 342 (in the Catalogue above quoted), the meeting at the Field of the Cloth of Gold; No. 407, Louis XIII., by Belcamp; No. 411, Marie de Medicis, by Pourbus; No. 418, Henry IV., by the same artist; No. 566, by Janet, of Francis I. and a lady, variously described as Diane de Poitiers, and as his wife Eleanor (No. 561), already mentioned; No. 582, La Belle Gabrielle; No. 592, a French nobleman, holding a copy of Petrarch, by Holbein, with long straight nose and narrow eyes, a close brown beard, black cape, and a low black round cap; No. 617, Marie de Lorraine, mother of the Queen of Scots, just misses being clever, and perhaps suffers by contrast with the magnificently beautiful portrait in No. 622.

At Hatfield the finest picture is the "Mary Queen of Scots," by P. Oudry, 1578; there is another of the same princess, in a Brabant costume, that is pretty but not authentic. Other paintings are François de Chatillon; Seigneur d'Andelot, a copy after Pourbus; Louise de Lorraine, Queen of Henry III.; Henry III., King of France, by F. Pourbus; Catherine de Medicis, a copy after Clouet; Henry, Duke of Guise, a copy, with a large and realistic scar on the left cheek; and Henry III., another copy, after F. Pourbus. The best examples of art at Hatfield are portraits which have no connection with the present subject.

The pictures with which we are concerned at Stafford House are all much finer. There are a good Henry III., Jeanne d'Albret, Catherine de Medicis, and François, Duc d'Alençon, all by François Clouet; and a Francis I., with his sister Marguerite, by Jean Clouet. At Castle Howard are other examples of the same school.

The portrait of Marie Stuart, reproduced in Chapter XIV., needs justification. Early in this century Alderman Fletcher gave the University of Oxford a duly authenticated portrait of Marie Stuart, of which coloured prints were afterwards published. Before the original was sent away to be cleaned, a copy was made, on the suggestion of Sir David Wilkie, which now exists in the Gallery of Bodley, together with a miniature copy of the original, presented by Miss Gutch. A copy by Jackson, which is now reproduced for the first time, was also made from the original in

1812. When the picture returned from the cleaner, an entirely different portrait was found to have appeared; the original has never been seen again. The chief beauty of Jackson's copy, the delicate colouring of the hair and eyes, is unavoidably absent in the reproduction, for which I am indebted to the kindness of Mr. A. Stowe of Wadham College, Oxford, who also furnished me with the details I have given of the picture's history.

The view of Chambord in Chapter XXI. is reproduced from an old collection of prints bound together in the Library of Wadham College. It is catalogued in the British Museum (the only other place where I know of its existence) as " *Veües des belles maisons de France* (les places, portes, fontaines, églises, et maisons de Paris; veües des plus beaux endroits de Versailles; diverses veües de Chantilly) designées et gravées par Perelle." (Paris, 1685, obl. 4to.) Brit. Mus. 564, f. 1. France, pt. 1, £ 136, b.

In conclusion, there are drawings by Étienne Delaulne in the Bodleian Library at Oxford, mentioned by Mrs. Mark Pattison. Among them occurs a profile of Marie Stuart, the reverse of a piece struck at the accession of her husband, Francis II. There are also coins for the reigns of Henry II., Francis II., Charles IX., and Henry III. The book is labelled as by Le Petit Bernard, and formed part of the Douce collection.

IV.—AUTHORITIES

It may be useful for purposes of reference to insert a few more authorities which have not been previously mentioned.

Among guide-books—*La Loire*, by Touchard Lafosse (1856), a large work in five volumes; *Touraine* (including a bibliography), by Bellanger; *Feudal Castles in France*, by Mrs. Byrne; *Historic Châteaux*, by A. B. Cochrane, M.P.; a *Handbook of Tours*, published in 1841; *La Cathédrale de Tours*, by Mgr. Chevalier; *Le Château de Chambord* and *Le Château de Blois*, by M. de la Saussaye; *Langeais*, by Maurice Brincourt, with drawings by Roy; *Loches*, by the Abbé E. Hat; *Le Château d'Amboise*, edited by M. Guilland Verger, Tours; *Lettre à M. de Caumont sur une Excursion en Touraine*, by M. de Cougny, and several other works by Mgr. Chevalier; *Fontevrault*, by M. Malifaud.

In periodical literature there has lately appeared an article on "Castle Life in the Middle Ages," in *Scribner's* for January 1889, by the two Blashfields, who contributed "The Paris of the Three Musketeers" to the same magazine for August 1890. In the *English Illustrated* for February 1891, "Thoughts in Prison," by Mrs. Watts Jones, contains a careful copy of nearly all the best inscriptions in Loches. In *Harper's* for June 1891 is a short article by Louis Fréchette on Blois, Chambord, and Amboise.

Of contemporary authorities, it has already been pointed out that the numerous works published under the auspices of the École des Chartes are of the highest value. For the Italian history, and much else of interest in the reigns of Louis XI. and Charles VIII., the history of Philippe de Commines has been used. Throughout, the works of Villon, Rabelais, Clement Marot, Ronsard, Regnier, Dumas, Balzac, De Vigny, and the pamphlets of P. L. Courier, illustrate in their own way the manner of the time. There is far more historically accurate matter in many of the novels of Dumas than he is often credited with; his fidelity, in particular, to the old *Mémoires* is astonishing, though he has not always so freely acknowledged the sources of his narratives as in

the reference to the *Mémoires* of the actual D'Artagnan
prefixed to his *Three Musketeers*. The picture of the
sixteenth century given in the older trilogy—*La Dame de
Montsoreau, La Reine Margot*, and *Les Quarante Cinq*—
is a very accurate one. *Les Deux Dianes* touches on
events in the reign of Henry II., and contains a vivid and
fairly true relation of the "Tumult of Amboise," which is
again described in Balzac's *Catherine de Medicis*. De
Vigny publishes with great care many of the manuscripts
and evidences for the story of the conspiracy of Cinq Mars
and De Thou, in his romance of *Cinq Mars*.

For the best idea of Mary Queen of Scots, the " Marie
Stuart " of French history, see the article on her life and
character in the *Encyclopædia Britannica*, which is perhaps
the finest piece of short biographical work ever written, and
has been republished, with an important additional note, in
Swinburne's *Miscellanies*, p. 323.

For further details as to the Abbé de Rancé, whose
" tragical history " was shortly sketched in Chapter XXIII.,
see the *Mémoires of the Count de Comminges*. As to the
Trappistes, see *Réglements de l'Abbaye de la Trappe*, par Dom
Armand de Rancé, and the narrative of Dom Claude Lancelot, 1667. Mr. W. D. Fellowes, in *A Visit to the Monastery of La Trappe* in 1817, etc., says that the inscription
on De Rancé's portrait there runs as follows :—" Mort en
1700 à près de 77 ans et de 40 ans (*sic*) de la plus austère
pénitence." This would give his age approximately at the
time of the episode mentioned in the text. The Monastery
of La Trappe is one of the most ancient abbeys of the order
of Benedictines, established in 1140 by Rotrou, Comte de
la Perche, as a thankoffering ; by 1660 its monks not only
lived in luxury, but were so famous for their scandalous
excesses of every kind, that they were called the Banditti

of La Trappe. It was to these men that De Rancé came and *reformed* the abbey (which he had the reputation of actually founding), by introducing the terribly austere rules for which the order is famous. De Rancé himself gives an interesting account of the first of the many visits of the unfortunate James II. to the Monastery in 1690. In Champfleury, *Histoire de la Caricature*, there is much interesting matter with reference not only to published sketches but to architecture, and even dramatic performances, during the period I have chiefly dealt with. In connection with these latter, he quotes a long passage from De Thou's *Mémoires* describing the entry of Francis II. into Tours after leaving Amboise ; both places, as we have seen, were famous for their *Mystery Plays* and allegorical representations, and on this occasion an imaginative baker equipped his son in a manner more likely to amuse the spectators than to gratify the Court : " tous disoient que cette représentation étoit une vive image de l'état du roy-aume, gouverné par un roi encore enfant, qui avoit pour ministres des étrangers qui l'avoient rendu aveugle." See also *La Satire en France au Moyen Age*, by C. Lenient ; and for another account of the beginning of the fifteenth century, which should have been mentioned earlier, see the edition by M. de Viriville of the *Chronique de la Pucelle*, by Guillaume Cousinot ; an earlier writer of the same name wrote the *Geste des nobles Francoys*, etc., MS. 10,297 in Bibl. Nat. The *Journal du Siège d'Orléans* in 1428 might also be added.

Passing to later authorities in the sixteenth century, the year 1588 almost claims a bibliography to itself. The most complete account of the murder of Guise, and the surrounding circumstances, is given by *François Miron Médecin du Roy Henry III*. Other authorities are the

Mémoires de l'Estoile, Sully's *Économies Royales*, and the *Chronologie Novennaire* of Palma Cayet. Further details will be found in "*Agréable Récit* de ce qui s'est passé aux dernières barricades de Paris," 1588; "*Nouvelles de la Cour*, escrites de Blois, Lundy dernier, dix septième jour d'Octobre," 1588 (which contains the election lists); "*Harangue prononcée par Monsieur de Bourges* aux trois estats assemblez au chasteau de Blois le jour saincte Catherine 25 Nov. à quatre heures du soir," 1588; "*Discours de ce qui est arrivé à Blois* jusques à la mort du duc et du Cardinal de Guise," 1588 (by a Protestant); *Le Martyre des deux Frères*, 1589 (by a Catholic). In *La Ligue*, by L. Vitet, vol. i. p. 320, are details of the exact costume of men and women at the time. More information may be found in the *Bibliographie* of Monod.

NOTE

As the "dernier mot" (in English) upon French art, I insert part of the speech of Sir Frederick Leighton to the students of the Royal Academy (*The Times*, 11th December 1891) :—

THE FRENCH RENAISSANCE

" And now we turn to a wholly new phase in French art, the expression of a new order of ideas and of materially altered social conditions. During the fourteenth and fifteenth centuries the prestige of the fighting nobility had suffered much through the introduction of artillery and the reverses of the English wars ; the middle classes, on the other hand, had, under the favour of the kings, steadily risen in importance. Before the end of the fifteenth century the printing press had begun to scatter knowledge far and wide. The discovery of a new continent across the Atlantic was stirring the imagination of the Old World. But it was a discovery within that Old World which was to exercise the deepest influence on the intellectual condition of France, the discovery of Italy, through the expeditions of Charles VIII. and Louis XII., for a discovery it may be called, though it must not be assumed that Italian influence was entirely absent in France until that period. Already in the middle of the fifteenth century, René of Anjou, himself a painter and the friend of the leading humanists of his time, had made his Court at Tarascon a centre of culture and of art, and employed the labour of Italian artists. Within the first half of the century, too, a great painter, Jehan Fouquet, had brought back from Italy a marked leaning to the new classic spirit. Nevertheless it was not until the return of the romantic stripling, Charles VIII., with the flower of the French nobility from his futile and fantastic campaign that the desire for all things Italian took wide and lasting hold of the French —at least, among the nobility—and this enthusiasm, further whetted during the chequered campaigns of his successor, Louis XII., grew at a rapid pace. It was not, however, till the second decade of the sixteenth century that, through the example of that brilliant dilettante, Francis I., the Italian contagion showed important results. Within the thirty-five years of his reign a host of palatial buildings were raised in a new style, which, if it had not, as had the style it pushed aside, the virtue of indigenous growth, was certainly marked by extreme charm and beauty. It was not, I say, of spontaneous growth, but neither was it a wholly alien product, for the people from whom it was adopted had in past times left on the more vivacious Gallic stock distinct traces of its blood, and the French have not ceased to this day to claim kinship with the Imperial race. Meanwhile, borrowed though the new style was, the French at once moulded it to their own genius, and produced a result distinctly personal to themselves ; and the modifications they introduced in the Italian style were just such as you would expect from the different temper of the race. The restrained and sweet gravity which delights us in the purest examples of trans-Alpine Renaissance is, it must be admitted, too often wanting in the French work of the same class ; and if, as I believe, the rank of a work of art is according to the dignity of the emotion it stirs in the beholder, then the creations of the great Italians rise to a higher level than those of the artists of the French Renaissance. For vitality and variety, on the other hand, for exuberance of fancy, for resourceful ingenuity of construction, and for a delicate sense of rhythm and proportion, the superiority of the work of the French is, in my opinion, conspicuous. Above all things, *it is their own*, and

for this reason it seems to me that the jealous investigation
which has been noticeable in recent times in France as to how
far Italian arts have been unduly credited with the building of
certain of the masterpieces of the Renaissance in that country
is, however valuable in the interests of truth, of no great
moment to the dignity of French art. Close study of documents has led, as is well shown, for instance, in Palustre's
beautiful instalment of a *History of French Renaissance*, to
the dismissal of claims hitherto advanced in various cases in
favour of Italian artists ; it is bringing into greater prominence
the names of native *maistres maçons* whose claims had been
underrated, men who had inherited traditions which made
them greatly superior, as builders at all events, to the artists
who came amongst them from beyond the Alps. But, apart
from such inquiries, it is patent that all but every work of the
French Early Renaissance, however it may have originated,
bears the unmistakable stamp of the fusing energy of French
genius. That the style was not born in France is a fact no
one can challenge ; that it was recast in that country into a
distinctly French thing no narrowness could dispute.

FRENCH DOMESTIC ARCHITECTURE

The keynote of the Renaissance movement being the asser-
tion of the beauty of life and the dignity of man, its influence
was naturally most felt in connection with secular life. The
great era of church building was past, and, indeed, for a
population reduced by long and wasting wars the existing
places of worship were not insufficient. The main determining
motive of artistic activity under Francis I. was the ambition of
the King and his nobles to multiply places of delight for their
residence, especially in the country, and to replace by sights of
beauty, such as they had learned to love and covet in Italy,
the moated gloom of their ancestral châteaux, built and well
suited for purposes of protection and defence, but little in

harmony with the tastes of the pleasure-loving Court and the light-hearted young King who led it. Prodigious and breathless was the activity with which châteaux were raised, first in the Royal province watered by the Loire, and then in and about Paris. It would be fruitless to enumerate at length even the chief of the stately buildings which from that time to the death of Henry III. occupied the energies of French architects ; nor can I do more here than name a few of the foremost of these considerable men, such as in the first line Jean Bullant and Philibert de l'Orme ; and in the second, Colin Biart, Pierre Chambiges, Pierre Nepveu, *alias* Trinqueau, Gadier, Le Prestre, and Hector Sohier. It will be more profitable to note a few points in connection with the evolution of the style itself. Although, as I have said, the great outburst of activity in the new direction coincides with the reign of Francis, Italian influence had already begun to assert itself in architecture as in other things in the preceding century, through Charles VIII., at Amboise, for instance, and more effectually under his successor, who built the east wing of the Château de Blois.

.✓   .   .   .   .

' In the case of secular buildings the transition from the later Gothic was facilitated by the fact that square-headed openings prevailed already in that style, of which, too, the incontinence in ornament was acceptable to the exuberant spirit of the new art. The character of that ornament, however, was entirely changed ; fantastic, foreign arabesque took the place of the floral decoration which had been one of the glories of the French school. Meanwhile the love for aspiring forms lived on, and the tendency to complexity died hard. The wealth of sky-line produced by spires and pinnacles was perpetuated in high-pitched roofs, turrets, and tall, buttressed dormer windows. The sky-line of Chambord could have been conceived only by an architect having Gothic tradition in his blood. In other matters, too, we find the Gothic habit surviving. The external winding staircase, for instance, was long preserved, and you may see on a dainty façade of the time of Francis I. the survival of the grouped shaft in a fanciful colonnette engaged on the face of a pilaster.

.   .   .   .

The days of civil strife and butchery in which so many noble lives were quenched in blood, the dark days of the Huguenot persecution, were not auspicious for the growth of art, and with the close of the century we find life and spontaneity at a low ebb — little production, a tendency now to heavy monotony and now to barocque redundancy, and a lack of sense and fitness which admitted of masking with a ponderous classic façade churches built on the scheme of, if not with the forms of, ogival architecture. Officialism, too, in artistic matters was at hand, and soon that implacable organiser Colbert was to regulate the arts, also by Royal decree, and to found an academy which admitted only one saving creed. The frigid pomp, the artificial graces of the structures inspired by the " Roi Soleil "—majestic in the many-storied wig which encircled his retreating brow—how far are they from the radiant daintiness, the joyous freedom of the palaces and pleasances which sprang up in the days and at the beck of that truly sunny Sovereign Francis I.!

OTHER ARTISTIC DEVELOPMENTS

To that period let us for one brief moment revert to notice, however summarily, the parallel development of painting and sculpture. In the latter art we have already recorded the names of Jean Goujon and Germain Pilon. These great artists were not without forerunners, of whom, no doubt, Michel Columbe was the most gifted, though his works lack both suppleness and definiteness of artistic purpose. I should name, also, Nicholas Bachelier and Giusti, the latter a family of Italians settled in Tours, but true to their nationality in the character of their work.

Turning now briefly to painting we find in the sixteenth century but little to rejoice us. Yet a few considerable names redeem it from bareness. When Francis I. began to build he did not find amongst his countrymen painters to whom he could entrust the decoration of his numerous palaces. The elder Clouet was, it is true, already prominently known, but both he and his more famous successor in the nickname of " Janet " were specially and exclusively painters of portraits. There were, of course, at the time a number of painters in the country ; but whilst it may be admitted that Francis, in his keen admiration for everything Italian, may in some measure have overlooked native talent, it is difficult to believe that any very marked personality could have failed to assert itself in spite of the crushing incubus of the Italian influence—a baneful influence, be it said in passing, for it was not the influence of Raphael or of Leonardo, of Andrea del Sarto or of Titian, with all of whom the King was in more or less direct contact, but the influence of Cellini, mischievous for all his genius—and especially, through their long sojourn in the country, that of Primaticcio, Il Rosso, and Nicolo dell' Abate, which weighed on the art of France. Nor does the sixteenth century in France boast in painting, apart from the Clouets, any name of much calibre, except perhaps that of Perréal, and certainly that of Jean Cousin, a man whose dignity of artistic temper preserved him in great measure from the excesses of the school of Parmigiano."

INDEX

THE END

Printed by R. & R. CLARK, *Edinburgh*